STEM Education Series

STEM Education
for Teachers by Student Teachers

Book Edited by

Pelin KONUK

Series Edited by

M. Sencer CORLU

Copyright © 2014 Task Force on STEM Education - FeTeMM Çalışma Grubu

All rights reserved.

ISBN: 1491074930

ISBN-13: 978-1491074930

CONTENTS

Foreword   Pg 4

1 The Concept of Sample Space in Probability   Pg 6

2 Exploring a Mysterious Number: the Golden Ratio   Pg 28

3 Archimedes' Principle: Buoyant Force   Pg 49

4 Sound   Pg 64

5 Power of Congruent Triangles   Pg 85

FOREWORD

Mary Margaret Capraro

Texas A&M University

"The belief that all genuine education comes about through experience does not mean that all experiences are genuinely or equally educative (Dewey, 1938, p. 25).

The advantage of implementing Science, Technology, Engineering, and Mathematics (STEM) activities in classrooms is the ability to include authentic tasks. These larger projects require students to work in groups to develop artifacts. This process is much closer to what is required in jobs. Therefore, future job success is increased through participation in these classroom activities. The interdisciplinary nature of STEM allows students to interact with knowledge across subjects rather than compartmentalize their learning into separate subject areas. Thus involvement in STEM allows students to engage in authentic tasks resulting in connecting learning from elementary, to middle, to high school and into post secondary education and ultimately into the workplace.

This book demonstrates the efforts of preservice teachers from Turkey and builds on the work of inservice teachers from the United States. The first book of this type was edited in 2010 by Capraro, Capraro, and Morgan entitled, *A companion to interdisciplinary STEM project-based learning: For teachers by teachers*. It was written by teachers and university partners in one school district after being involved in a series of professional developments through Texas A&Ms' Aggie STEM, a State of Texas center. The teachers who were involved in the first book did not graduate from college with these experiences and knowledge, they gained it after school and on Saturdays. The preservice teachers who wrote the lesson plans in this book had the opportunity to learn during a course they took during their post secondary instruction, taught to them by Dr. M. Sencer Corlu who is a former graduate student with the Aggie STEM center. The areas of probability, the golden ratio, buoyancy, sound, and congruent triangles are focused on but many other objectives are covered through the connections to other topics and subject areas. Just as the lessons in the first book are not expected to be exact lesson plans for teachers who pick up the book, this book is a collection of lessons that can be adapted for individual classrooms. The authors of this book welcome your ideas and suggestions as you implement the adapted lessons in your classrooms.

AUTHORS

Melih Akar

Osman Canavar

Gizem Yeter Bas

Hilal Köksal

Yasemin Çiçek

BOOK EDITOR

Pelin Konuk is a graduate student, pursuing her initial teacher training at Bilkent University.

An e-book version is available to download from http://fetemm.org

1 THE CONCEPT OF SAMPLE SPACE IN PROBABILITY

INTRODUCTION

A sample space is the set of all possible outcomes of an experiment. It is used to calculate the probabilities of an experiment in both mathematics and real–life situations. In this chapter, students are exposed to probabilistic activities and asked to calculate the sample spaces of given situations. In addition, the chapter explores probability and hence sample space usage in science. The lessons are mainly activity based and student centered.

OBJECTIVES

Mathematics

– Students are expected to construct sample spaces using lists.

Science

– Students are expected to recognize that inherited traits of individuals are governed in the genetic material found in the genes within chromosomes in the nucleus.

Technology

– Students are expected to use appropriate software components which are suitable for the task.

– Students are expected to use technology applications to facilitate their work.

MATERIALS

– Computer for each group

– Worksheet 1

– Worksheet 2

– LCD projector to show videos

STUDENT INTRODUCTION

Have you ever gambled on horse races or played the lottery? Have you ever gained money from such activities? What are your chances of winning in those activities? There are so many people who engage in those activities every year all over the world. Any situation that involves chance or probability is called an experiment. The set of all possible outcomes in such an activity is called a sample space. As you can easily predict, if the number of outcomes increases, then the probability of winning in those activities decreases. In other words, if the number of outcomes in a sample space is high, then the probability of guessing the winning result is low. The concept of sample space is the key component in finding the likelihood of a probability experiment. In the later parts of probability study, in order to determine the probability we need to calculate the sample space. Otherwise, the probability of an event cannot be determined. In the subsequent lessons, we will go into the concept of sample space, what it means, and how to calculate it.

ENGAGEMENT

Before starting this activity, the teacher divides the students into teams of two to perform an activity. Then, he or she gives each group two urns. The first urn contains ten red and five blue marbles, and the second urn contains ten red and twenty blue marbles. Then, the teacher asks the students to pick five marbles from each urn and record the results. One student picks the marbles and the other student records the results. After students perform all picking and recording, the teacher asks in which urn it is more likely to pick a blue marble. Then, the teacher asks the students to discuss the question by linking it to what they have recorded. This part simply intends to develop a brief understanding of the concept of sample space and to encourage students to think a little bit about the sample space. Together with a teacher–led discussion, this part takes approximately one hour.

EXPLORATION

In this stage, the teacher helps students to explore the meaning of sample space. The teacher divides the students into teams of four. Each group performs the activity independently. Before starting the activity, the teacher provides some introductory information and asks some thought–provoking questions. For example, he or she should ask questions such as which cell has the highest occurrence rate. Such questions might direct students to think more sensitively and appropriately for developing an understanding of the logic of probability. Overall, the activity consists of two parts. In the first part, students have six prisoners whom they are trying to release. Students roll two dice, calculate the difference, and release the prisoner if that number is one. In addition, questions are stated in the second part that are important, because they include guiding questions that lead students through an initial exploration of the concept of sample space. For this reason, the teacher should not let students skip any questions.

Release the Prisoners Game. Worksheet 1

In this first part of the game, you have six prisoners, whom you want to release.

Game Rules

– You have six prisoners and six cells; you are free to choose how to place the prisoners into the cells.

– You are not obligated to place the six prisoners into different cells. You can place all of them into one cell, you can distribute all of them into different cells, and so on.

– You have two dice. Roll them, calculate the difference, and release one of your prisoners, if that number is one.

– There are two other people performing the same activity. The first to release all of his or her prisoners in the given time interval is the winner.

– Good luck!

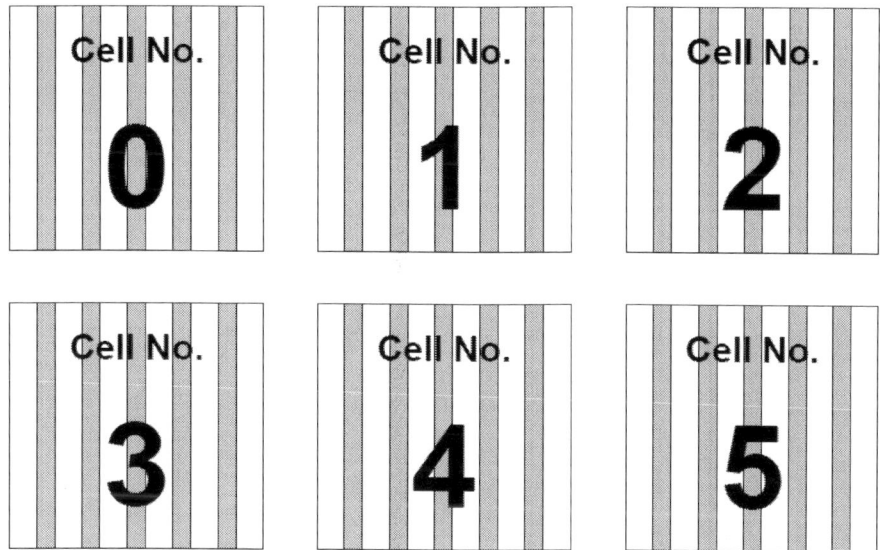

Release the Prisoners Game. Worksheet 2

In this part of the game, you have five questions to answer. Answer them carefully.

1. Is the game fair? What do you think? Explain your answer in a few sentences.

2. Who is the most successful person in your group? Why is that person the best? Is he or she very lucky, or is there another reason behind his or her success?

3. Could choosing the numbers that have the highest frequency or occurrence rate be a reason for the best player's success?

4. If you were to replay the game, which numbers would you choose in both parts?

5. Can you make a list of all the outcomes that can be drawn in both cases? What do we call it?

After students perform the activity, the teacher starts a discussion about the students' findings and then asks those who did not win about their failure. In this way, the teacher gets the students to query themselves to give them a chance to learn from their failure. This provides a step–by–step exploration of the notion of sample space.

EXPLANATION

First, the teacher asks students to make a tabular representation of the results of rolling two dice. In so doing, students have a chance to look at the entire sample space and see the mistakes that they made in the first part of the activity. The teacher initially asks the students to find the results of rolling two coins and then asks them to calculate the difference of the numbers in the sample space, as was required in the first part of the activity.

Table 1

	1	2	3	4	5	6
1	(1,1)	(1,2)	(1,3)	(1,4)	(1,5)	(1,6)
2	(2,1)	(2,2)	(2,3)	(2,4)	(2,5)	(2,6)
3	(3,1)	(3,2)	(3,3)	(3,4)	(3,5)	(3,6)
4	(4,1)	(4,2)	(4,3)	(4,4)	(4,5)	(4,6)
5	(5,1)	(5,2)	(5,3)	(5,4)	(5,5)	(5,6)
6	(6,1)	(6,2)	(6,3)	(6,4)	(6,5)	(6,6)

Table 2

	1	2	3	4	5	6
1	0	1	2	3	4	5
2	1	0	1	2	3	4
3	2	1	0	1	2	3
4	3	2	1	0	1	2
5	4	3	2	1	0	1
6	5	4	3	2	1	0

In the table, the teacher shows students that one is the most frequently occurring number, with ten occurrences in the sample space. Two is the second most frequent number, with eight occurrences, three and zero are third, with six occurrences, four is fourth, with four occurrences, and five is the least frequent, with two occurrences. If the students had thought to make this tabularization or at least to imagine the picture beforehand, they would have had better results.

Now they understand better the meaning of sample space. Then, the teacher asks the students to visit the web page located at http://sciencenetlinks.com/media/filer/2011/10/13/marblemania.swf to open the Marble Mania! activity. Directing this activity is very easy.

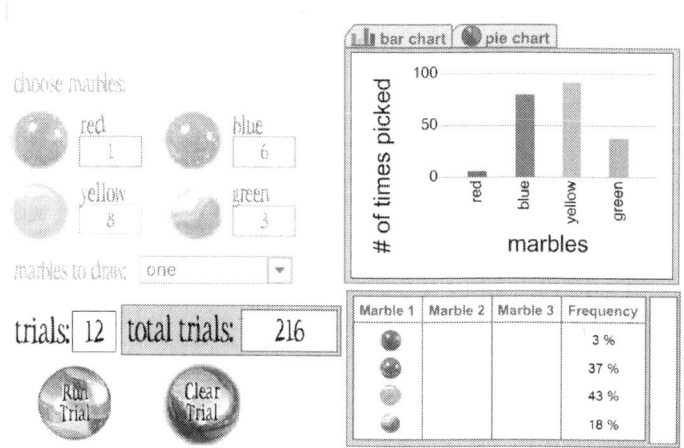

Students can increase the number of marbles and, hence, change the sample space. The teacher asks the students to determine the number of marbles and then to start the trial. There are two options, such as a bar chart and a pie chart. Students should be allowed to determine the type of chart. For example, let us perform a trial: choose one red, six blue, eight yellow, and three green marbles, so there are 18 marbles in our sample space. The bulk of the marbles are blue and yellow, so we can presume that more than half of the marbles drawn from the file would be blue or yellow. At this point, students should derive that conclusion. If they do not, the teacher reviews the previous activity. Then, the teacher shows a video about Mendel's laws on the web page located at

http://www.bbc.co.uk/schools/gcsebitesize/science/add_aqa/inheritance/genetic_variationact.shtml

The video is about the genes in the human body that come from the father and mother. Having brown eyes is dominant in the sample space. The teacher briefly goes over the details.

Gregor Johann Mendel was an Austrian scientist and cleric who achieved posthumous fame as the founder of the new science of genetics. He was a gardener who worked with peas. Mendel studied the alleles that come from chromosomes.

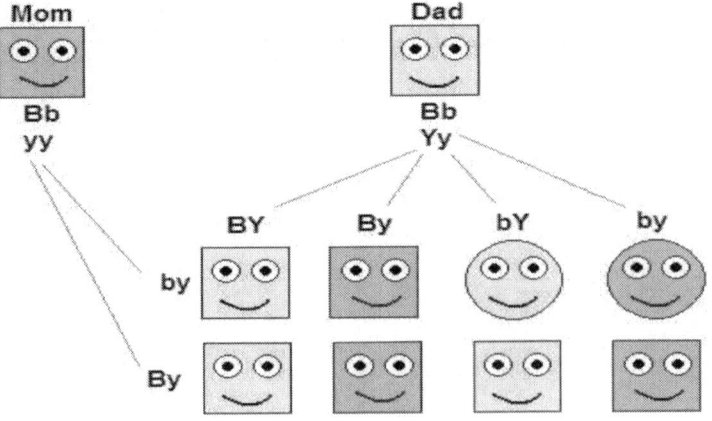

Figure 1. Crossing the alleles coming from the parents

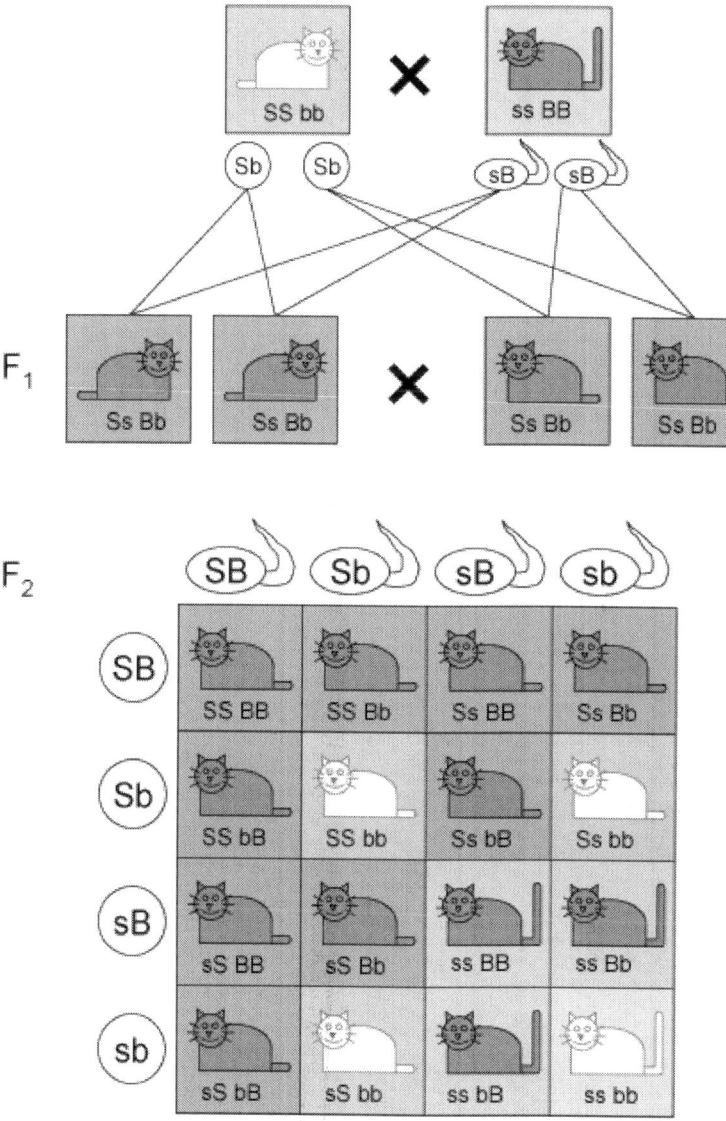

Figure 2. An example of crossing in cats

Using tree diagrams to find the sample space: The teacher asks the students for the sample space of flipping two coins. The students have already seen the sample space, so getting the correct results should not be difficult. Then, the teacher shows the tree diagram of tossing two coins.

STEM Education: For Teachers by Student Teachers

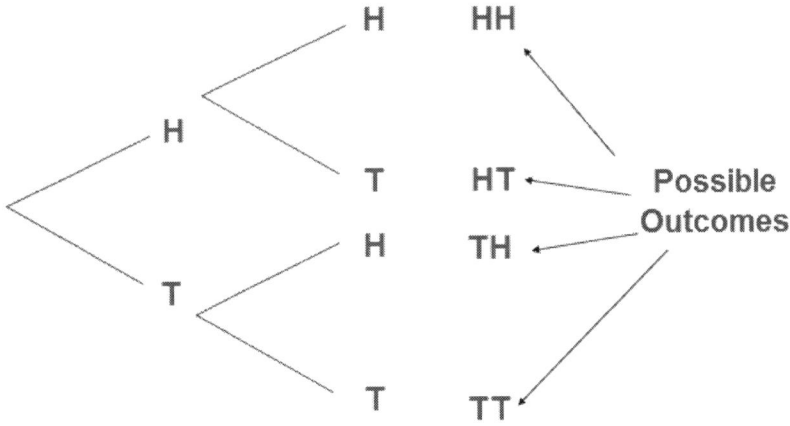

Figure 3. Tree diagram of flipping two coins

Next, the teacher explains the construction of tree diagrams using different examples, as follows:

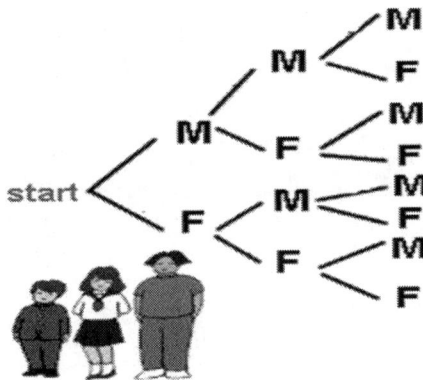

Figure 4. Children in a family

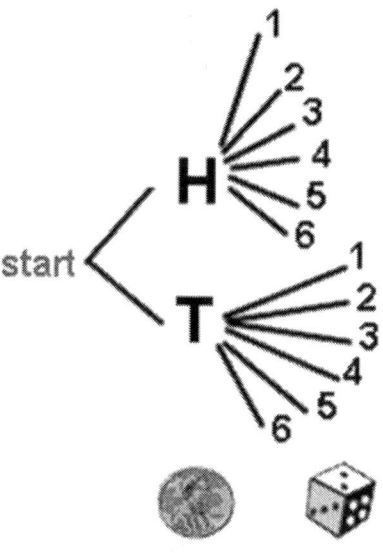

Figure 5. Tossing a coin and rolling a die

EXTENTION

The teacher opens a stick or switch activity from Utah State University's library of virtual manipulatives. This is an entertaining activity that tests students' knowledge of the concept of sample space. In the activity, there are three doors, only one of which is the winning one. Here is a picture of what it looks like:

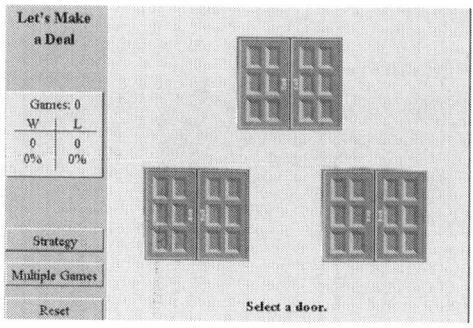

Figure 6. Stick or switch activity

The strategy of the game is simple. There are three doors, and we want to find the winning one. However, two trials are offered to find the winning door. First, we choose a door. Then the program opens another door, so we have the two options of either sticking with the same door or switching the door. The teacher asks students to find the strategy that produces the most productive outcome.

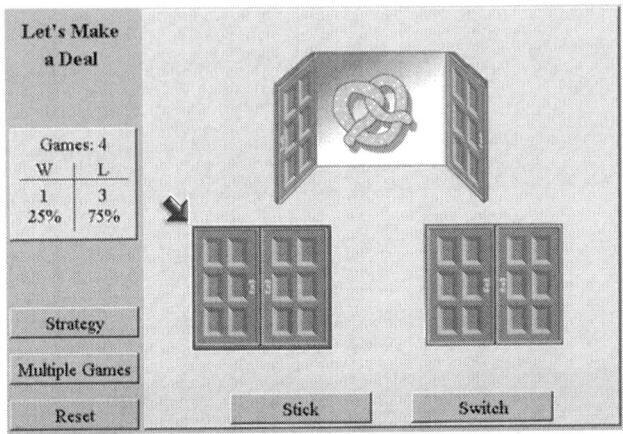

Figure 7. Stick or switch activity

The picture shows how the activity looks after one trial. The program shows two doors, one of which is a losing door, and offers two options, stick or switch.

Hint: Use a tree diagram to list all of the outcomes to determine what strategy is most useful for winning most of the time.

EVALUATION

True or False

Circle the correct answer.

1. A sample space is a set of all possible outcomes. [True/False]

2. The sample space of a tossing–a–coin activity consists of six elements. [True/False]

3. In a tossing–two–coins activity, the sample space contains four elements. [True/False]

4. If we remove a possible outcome from the set of all possible outcomes, the sample space does not change. [True/False]

5. With two four–sided dice, the sample space of the experiment of tossing two dice consists of eight elements. [True/False]

6. In a rolling–two–dice–experiment, the sample space consists of 36 elements. [True/False]

7. There are 3 blue, 5 purple, 6 green, and 12 white marbles in an urn. The sample space of drawing a marble from the urn has 26 outcomes. [True/False]

8. When we roll a die and toss a coin, then the sample space consists of 12 outcomes. [True/False]

9. The sample space of the tossing–four–coins experiment contains 16 outcomes. [True/False]

10. A tree diagram is a tool that is used to show all possible outcomes of an activity. [True/False]

Answer Sheet

1) T, 2) F, 3) T, 4) F, 5) F, 6) T, 7) T, 8) T, 9) T, 10) T

Short Answer

1. What is the term that means a situation involving chance or probability and producing results called outcomes?

2. What do we call the set {1, 2, 3, 4, 5, 6} in a coin tossing experiment?

3. What are the symbols that we use to show a sample space?

4. What is the name of a circle with an arrow in the center that turns along the circular path?

5. What would be the number of outcomes in a tossing–a–coin–and–rolling–a–die experiment?

Answer Sheet

1. Experiment

2. Sample Space

3. S, Ω, or U

4. Spinner

5. 12

Multiple–Choice Questions

1. What is the sample space for choosing an odd number from one to ten at random?

a. 1, 2, 3, 4, 5, 6, 7, 8, 9, 10

b. {1, 2, 3, 4, 5, 6, 7, 8, 9, 10}

c. {1, 3, 5, 7, 9}

d. {2, 4, 6, 8, 10}

2. What is the sample space for choosing a prime number less than 13 at random?

a. {2, 3, 5, 7, 11, 13}

b. 2, 3, 5, 7, 11, 13

c. {2, 3, 5, 7, 9, 11, 13}

d. {1, 3, 5, 7, 9}

3. What is the sample space for choosing one jelly marble at random from a jar containing five red, seven blue, and two green jelly marbles?

a. {5, 7, 2}

b. {5 red, 7 blue, 2 green}

c. {red, blue, green}

d. {5 red, 7 blue}

4. What is the sample space for choosing one consonant at random from the word 'Space'?

a. {S, P, C}

b. {S, P, A, C, E}

c. {A, E}

d. {S, P, C, E}

5. What is the number of possible outcomes from drawing a card from a deck?

a. 52

b. 51

c. 13

d. 15

6. What is the sample space if two coins are tossed?

a. {T, H}

b. {T, T}

c. {H, H}

d. {(T, T), (T, H), (H, T), (H, H)}

7. What is the sample space if a coin is rolled?

a. {1, 2, 3, 4, 5, 6}

b. {1, 3, 4, 5, 6}

c. {1, 2, 3, 5, 6}

d. {0, 1, 2, 3, 4, 5}

8. In a jar there are three blue, two red, and six purple marbles. A marble is drawn from the jar, and we know the color of the marble is not blue. In this sense, what would be the new sample space for this experiment?

a. {3 blue, 2 red, and 6 purple}

b. {2 red and 6 purple}

c. {3 blue, 2 red}

d. {3 blue and 6 purple}

9. If the sample space of an experiment is {(T, T), (T, H), (H, T), (H, H)}, then what could be the experiment?

a. Tossing two coins

b. Tossing a coin and rolling a die

c. Rolling a die and drawing a card from a deck

d Tossing two coins

10. A box contains tickets numbered from one to 15. John picks a ticket and says the number on the ticket is not odd. Then, according to John's statement, what would be the sample space?

a. {1, 2, 3, 4, 5, 6, 7}

b. {2, 3, 5, 7, 11, 13}

c. {2, 4, 6, 8, 10, 12, 14}

d. {1, 3, 5, 7, 9, 11, 13, 15}

11. If the sample space of an experiment is {5 red, 7 blue, 2 green}, then what could be the experiment?

a. Drawing a card from a deck

b. Picking a marble from jar that contains five red, seven blue, and two green marbles

c. Drawing a ticket from a container that contains seven blue and seven red tickets

d. Rolling a die and tossing a coin

12. What is the sample space of the experiment if we want to pick a vowel from the letters of the word 'Turkey'?

a. {T, R, K}

b. {U, E}

c. {T, R, K, Y}

d. {T, U, R, K}

13. What is the number of outcomes in the experiment if we want to draw a vowel from the word 'Mississippi'?

a. 1

b. 11

c. 4

d. 7

14. What is the sample space if two coins are tossed and we know the faces come up the same?

a. {(T, T), (H, H)}

b. {(H, H)}

c. {(T, T), (H, H), (H, T)}

d. {(T, T), (T, H), (H, T), (H, H)}

15. What is the sample space of tossing two coins if the sum of the numbers that come up is six?

a. {(1, 4), (1, 5), (2, 4), (1, 6)}

b. {(1, 4), (1, 4), (1, 4), (1, 4)}

c. {(2, 4), (1, 5), (3, 3), (4, 2), (5, 1)}

d. {(3, 4), (3, 3)}

Answer Sheet

1) B, 2) C, 3) B, 4) A, 5) A, 6) D, 7) A, 8) B, 9) D, 10) C, 11) B, 12) C, 13) C, 14) A, 15) C

ALTERNATIVE ASSESSMENT

Task 1: The Horse Race Problem

In a horse race, there are five horses, named Hansen, Gemologist, Prospective, Liaison, and Padrino. According to the rules of the race, whoever guesses the first three horses correctly wins $500. You can make only one bet on a ticket. For example, you could select Hansen as the first horse, Gemologist as the second, and Padrino as the third. A ticket costs $10. You want to calculate all possible results of the race and bet on each one to be sure of winning the race to get the $500. How many choices must you make to be sure of winning the race? How much money will it cost? Is it rational to invest that much money in the race? Solve the problem and explain your ideas explicitly.

Hint: Make a tree diagram to calculate all possible outcomes of the horse race.

Rubric 1: The Horse Race Problem

	Understanding the problem	Planning a solution	Getting an answer
4–3	Students fully understand the problem and linked it to the concept of sample space.	Students use the rules for constructing tree diagrams smoothly and properly.	A tree diagram of all of the possibilities of the race is drawn without error, the number of outcomes is counted, the total price is calculated, and the correct inference about investing the money is drawn.
2–1	The problem is misunderstood or lacks some features relating to the sample space concept.	Students fail to use the rules that are mentioned in class to construct tree diagrams efficiently.	An incomplete tree diagram results in the sample space of the race not being finished, there are errors in counting the number of elements in the sample space, or faulty inferences are drawn about investing $500 in the game.
0	The problem is totally misunderstood.	No strategy or an incorrect strategy is followed to handle the problem.	There is no tree diagram or an incorrect one, the number of outcomes in the sample space is calculated incorrectly, or an incorrect inference or no inference is drawn.

Task 2: Names of the Children in a Family

Suppose a family has four children, all of them boys, named Jack, Adam, Adriano, and George. The brothers are born in successive years. What are all possible choices for the names of the children from the eldest to the youngest? For example, here is one possible order: {Jack, Adam, Adriano, George}. In this order, the eldest boy is named Jack, and the youngest is named George. Likewise, the second child is Adam, and the third is Adriano. Make a list of all possible outcomes, and state the method and the strategy you use to calculate all possible outcomes.

Rubric 2: Names of the Children in a Family

	Understanding the problem	Planning a solution	Getting an answer
4–3	The children problem is totally understood, and students refer it to the sample space concept.	Students use an efficient plan to solve the problem, and make efficient use of the rules mentioned in class to draw a tree diagram.	Students correctly calculate all possible outcomes with reference to the ages of the children in the problem.
2–1	The problem is only partially understood or is misunderstood, or the link between the question and the sample space is not established.	Students do not use an efficient strategy to calculate the number of outcomes.	Students miss some of the required calculations, or some of the boys' names are wrong.
0	Students completely misunderstand the problem.	Examples or methods given in the lecture are not used to solve the problem, or no strategy is followed.	The answer is missing or totally wrong.

Task 3: Dice Differences Activity

Suppose two friends play a game. Let us call them player A and player B. In the game, they roll two dice in turn and calculate the difference between the two dice. If the result is equal to zero, one, or two, then player A makes a mark on the table, and if the result is three, four, or five, then player B makes a mark on the table. The one who reaches ten marks first will be the winner. Is the game fair? What do you think? Answer this question by listing all possible outcomes of rolling two dice in a table. Then, make another table that shows the differences in numbers of each possible solution. For example, the cell (6, 1) corresponds to the cell 5 in the second table. After you construct the second table, paint the differences in which player A draws the tic. Construct your tables on paper, and then explain your ideas about the fairness of the activity with rational ideas that are linked to the percentages of the differences that each player has for making a mark.

Rubric 3: Dice Differences Activity

	Understanding the problem	**Planning a solution**	**Getting an answer**
4–3	Students understand the problem completely, and students see the unfairness in the activity.	Students apply the suggested method to solve the question step by step.	Tables are completed, the sample space of rolling two dice is correctly defined, and the activity's unfairness is supported with valid reasoning.
2–1	Part of the problem is misunderstood or misinterpreted.	Students try to follow the method suggested for the problem, but deviate at some points.	Errors occur in calculating the sample space, mistakes occur in constructing the tables, or the unfairness of the activity is explored but not explained elegantly or rationally.
0	Students completely misunderstand the problem.	The road map suggested in the question is not followed, or there is no strategy or plan to solve the question.	No sample space is given, the tables are missing, or nearly all of the items are wrong.

Rubric 4 (Extension Activity)

	Developing a strategy to win most of the time.
4	The sample space of the given chance game is completely explained, using that strategy students reach the result changing to what would be the most beneficial for winning most of the time, and ideas are supported with valid reasoning.
3	The sample space is given correctly, students reach the result changing to what would be the most beneficial for winning most of the time, but ideas are not supported with valid reasoning.
2	The sample space is correctly found, but students cannot conclude that changing would be most beneficial for winning most of the time, or ideas are not supported with valid reasoning.
1	Calculation of the sample space includes errors, students cannot conclude that changing would be most beneficial for winning most of the time, or ideas are not supported with valid reasoning.
0	Very little or no effort is exerted even to find the sample space.

AUTHOR

Melih Akar

Primary Education Department

Boğaziçi University

2 EXPLORING A MYSTERIOUS NUMBER: THE GOLDEN RATIO

INTRODUCTION

The golden ratio is an irrational number equal to 1.618033988749895… (up to 15 digits after the decimal point). It is a mysterious number that can be seen in almost all living organisms throughout the world. As we will see later, it is defined in terms of a ratio, so it is referred to most of the time as the golden ratio rather than the golden number. Yet, there are also people who call it the golden number. According to Benavoli (2009), the first mathematical definition of the golden ratio was introduced by the Greek mathematician Euclid. Euclid introduced it after solving a geometrical problem called division of a line segment in extreme and mean ratio. The meaning of this is as follows: Let us assume a line segment that consists of two parts whose lengths are different. In other words, the line segment is made up of two line segments, one smaller and the other larger. Division of a line in extreme and mean ratio means that the result of dividing the length of the larger part by the length of the smaller part is equal to the result of dividing the total length of the line segment by the length of the larger part. That ratio is called the golden ratio. That is the original definition of the golden ratio. However, this chapter starts with a different property of the golden ratio. First, the chapter introduces the Fibonacci sequence introduced by Leonardo Pisano; later, we will see that the ratio of consecutive terms in the sequence gives the golden ratio as the number of terms in the sequence increases. As the lesson progresses, the students will explore this ratio in the sequence using online software, and they will have an opportunity to look at situations, especially in nature, in which the golden ratio appears.

OBJECTIVES

Mathematics

– Students start to make use of patterns, relationships and algebraic reasoning. Students are expected to select to use appropriate forms of rational and irrational numbers to determine the ratio of the numbers in a given set of numbers.

— Students are expected to employ their algebraic reasoning to describe the relationship between the terms in a non–arithmetic sequence.

Technology

— Students illustrate the use of suitable software components and they are expected to utilize technology terminology appropriate to the task.

— Students demonstrate the ways information acquisition and they are expected to use technology applications to facilitate evaluation of work, both process and product.

Science

— Students make use of scientific investigation and reasoning. Students are expected to use models to represent aspects of the natural world such as human body systems and plants.

MATERIALS

— One computer per student with internet access

— An LCD projector

— Worksheets that include questions stated in the evaluation part

STUDENT INTRODUCTION   DNA

How would you feel if I told you that different parts of your body are proportional? The ratio of the part above your elbow and the part below your elbow is equal for all of you. Actually, it is not true just for you, but for all human beings in the world, including your mom, your sister, your grandmother, and of course, me. The same ratio holds approximately in all human beings. In addition, the ratio is not only seen in the construction of your arm; it appears in all parts of your body such as your legs, your face, your fingers, and so on. However, more interesting than that is that the another ratio appears in nature. For example, in the body sections of insects, in the dimensions of fins, in the structures of cones and sunflowers, and in infinitely many areas that you can imagine, the same ratio manifests itself. The aforementioned ratio is called the golden ratio or the golden number. The golden number is symbolized with the Latin letter Φ (phi), and its value is approximately 1.618. There have been many research studies relating to this number, with many interesting findings. Since the same ratio exists in many distinct areas of human life, it directly concerns human life. One of the findings, for example, is that the golden ratio is accepted as the 'ratio of beauty'. Thus, if you design an object with a rectangular shape that you intend to be attractive, the longer side of the rectangle should be Φ times larger than the smaller side.

ENGAGEMENT

To look at those distinct areas and to get some information about the nature of the golden ratio, let us watch the video on the web site located at http://www.youtube.com/watch?v=aB_KstBiou4

After the students have watched the video, the teacher starts a discussion about their ideas about what they have watched. This part is important for attracting students' attention to the subject. Another helpful video is available at the web site located at http://www.youtube.com/watch?v=U2bAlIK4KkE

The two videos contain some common parts, so the teacher can skip those parts. The two videos together last nearly ten minutes, and in total, the teacher should enrich the discussion and elaborate the lesson to the end of a class hour. The problem is the following:

Fibonacci Rabbits

"Suppose you have a pair of rabbits. We know that a pair of rabbits cannot bear offspring until they are two months old. However, once they become mature enough, they produce a pair of rabbits each month. If you are given a pair of new–born rabbits in the beginning, how many pairs of rabbits will you have at the beginning of each of the following months?"

At the first step, the teacher asks the students to determine the terms of the sequence. Of course, they cannot write the whole set, because the terms go to infinity. The teacher really wants the students to find the pattern by which the terms of the sequence can be determined. In other words, the teacher expects that the students will explore what rule the terms of the sequence follow. For those students who perform the first step, the teacher directs them to test whether would there be a ratio between the terms of the sequence. Since many computations must be performed at this point, the teacher should let the students use calculators. This part of the study lasts approximately one class hour. For those students who struggle to explore the two steps, some extra assistance from the teacher may be necessary.

EXPLANATION

Before beginning this stage, the teacher assigns one computer to each group. Each group should have a computer with Internet access. In the flow of this part, a computer is needed. First, the teacher shows a table of the solution to the problem. The table shows the number of pairs of rabbits at the beginning of each of the first five months.

Month	Pairs of Rabbits	Total Pairs
1	🐇	1
2	🐇	1
3	🐇🐇	2
4	🐇🐇🐇	3
5	🐇🐇🐇🐇🐇	5

Figure 1. Number of pairs of rabbits in each of the first five months

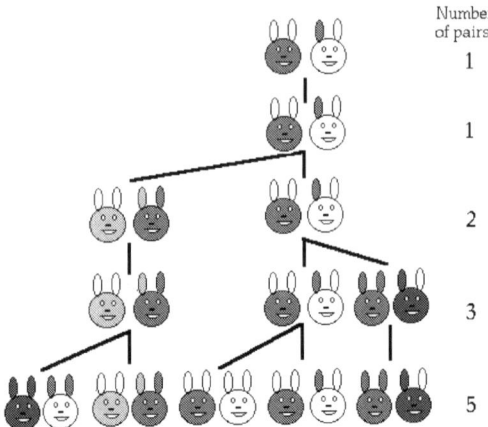

Figure 2. Alternative representation of Fibonacci rabbits

By looking at the table, the students can see how rabbits reproduce and increase, and that the number of rabbits forms the terms of the Fibonacci sequence. Then, the teacher asks the students to open a spreadsheet file and use the program to see some number of Fibonacci terms. Microsoft Excel is preferred, because most students are familiar with it. After the students open Microsoft Excel, the teacher asks them to write the first two Fibonacci terms in two rows of a column. For example, students write 1 in both E1 and E2. Next, the teacher asks the students to click E3, write the formula = E1 + E2, and press the Enter button. Then the students will see 2 in E3. To calculate automatically as many terms as desired, the program is instructed to evaluate the formula at least two times. This means students write the formula to find the fourth term. After they write the formula twice, they can drag by clicking E3 to apply the formula automatically to find the successive terms. Here is a picture of many Fibonacci terms calculated with Microsoft Excel.

B	C	D	E	F	G	H
			1			
			1			
			2			
			3			
			5			
			8			
			13			
			21			
			34			
			55			
			89			
			144			
			233			
			377			
			610			
			987			
			1597			
			2584			
			4181			
			6765			
			10946			
			17711			
			28657			
			46368			
			75025			
			121393			
			196418			

Figure 3. Fibonacci terms found from Microsoft Excel

Utah State University has a library of virtual manipulatives. The teacher asks the students to visit the web site that contains those virtual manipulatives located at http://nlvm.usu.edu/.

Next, the teacher asks the students to click the Number and Operations part and find the manipulative labeled Fibonacci Sequence. This is a virtual, online tool for seeing the Fibonacci terms and the ratios between consecutive terms. The tool is very easy to use. There is a button located at the bottom of the page for seeing the consecutive terms and the ratios between them. Here is a screenshot of the first five terms with the ratios of consecutive terms:

Fibonacci Sequence

$F_1 = 1$ $F_2 = 1$ $F_{n+1} = F_n + F_{n-1}$

n	1	2	3	4	5
F_n	1	1	2	3	5
$\dfrac{F_{n+1}}{F_n}$	$\dfrac{1}{1}$	$\dfrac{2}{1}$	$\dfrac{3}{2}$	$\dfrac{5}{3}$	$\dfrac{8}{5}$
	1.00000000	2.00000000	1.50000000	1.66666666	1.60000000

Golden Ratio = $\dfrac{1+\sqrt{5}}{2}$ = 1.618033988...

Figure 4. First five Fibonacci terms with the ratios of consecutive terms

When we look at the ratios of the first five pairs of consecutive terms, the numbers are close to the golden ratio, but they are not as close as we would like. Thus, we click the >> button to see the following terms. Here are the next five terms:

Fibonacci Sequence

$F_1 = 1$ $F_2 = 1$ $F_{n+1} = F_n + F_{n-1}$

n	6	7	8	9	10
F_n	8	13	21	34	55
$\dfrac{F_{n+1}}{F_n}$	$\dfrac{13}{8}$	$\dfrac{21}{13}$	$\dfrac{34}{21}$	$\dfrac{55}{34}$	$\dfrac{89}{55}$
	1.62500000	1.61538461	1.61904761	1.61764705	1.61818181

Golden Ratio = $\dfrac{1+\sqrt{5}}{2}$ = 1.618033988...

Figure 5. Second five Fibonacci terms with the ratios of consecutive terms

The ratio between the tenth term and the ninth term is very close to the golden ratio. This is want we want to observe about the terms of the Fibonacci sequence.

Golden Ratio in Nature

The golden ratio can be observed in many areas in nature. For example, a plant takes the following shape while it is growing. The teacher shows the picture and how the leaves form the Fibonacci terms and hence the golden ratio.

Figure 6. Fibonacci terms in plants

Then, the teacher asks the students to visit the web site located at http://www.maths.surrey.ac.uk/hosted-sites/R.Knott/Fibonacci/fibnat.html#seeds and to look at the sunflower.

There are buttons on the right hand side of the sunflower labeled Show right spirals, Show left spirals, and No spirals. The teacher asks the students to click the left–spirals button and see what happens.

Figure 7. Left spirals on sunflower

Next, the teacher asks the students to click the right–spirals button. Actually, the sums of the seeds that lie on both the right and left sides give us the Fibonacci terms. The teacher asks the students to count those seeds and record the results. Then, the students explore how a sunflower is related to the golden ratio. Now, after exploring how the golden ratio appears in the sunflower, the teacher asks the students to visit the web site located at http://www.homeschoolmath.net/teaching/fibonacci_golden_section.php

and click the Pine cones button. There are similar buttons at the bottom of the photograph of the pine cones. The teacher asks the students to click those buttons and observe the results.

EXTENSION

The teacher asks the students to visit the web page located at http://www.mathsisfun.com/numbers/nature-golden-ratio-fibonacci.html
and scroll down to the middle of the page, where the students will see the Turn and Grow virtual manipulative. The teacher asks the students to enter different values around the golden ratio and observe how spirals appear. The teacher lets the students observe the spirals and how the shape of the spirals begins to look like the distribution of the seeds in a sunflower. Here are some examples:

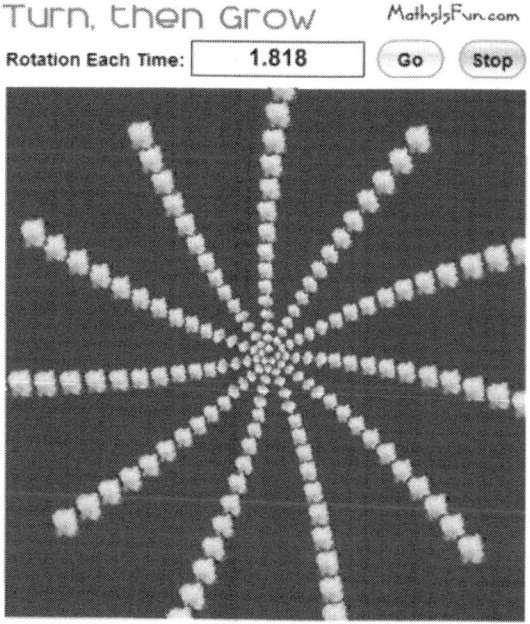

Figure 8. Rotation by 1.818

After doing this, the students are asked to write a short paper about their understanding and interpretation of what they have observed and, in particular, why the rotation around the golden ratio produces the shape of a sunflower.

EVALUATION

True and False

Circle the correct answer.

1. The number 1.618 is called the golden ratio. [True/False]

2. The golden ratio was first introduced by the Greek Mathematician Pythagoras. [True/False]

3. One definition of the golden ratio is that it is the ratio for which the larger part of a line segment divided by the smaller part is equal to the total divided by the larger part. [True/False]

4. The Fibonacci sequence was discovered by Leonardo Pisano. [True/False]

5. In the Fibonacci rabbits problem, there are five pairs of rabbits at the beginning of the fifth week. [True/False]

6. The ratio of two adjacent terms in the Fibonacci sequence is called the golden ratio. [True/False]

7. The ratio between the first two Fibonacci terms is equal to 1.618. [True/False]

8. The golden ratio is seen only in the human body. [True/False]

9. The tenth Fibonacci term is 55. [True/False]

10. In the Fibonacci sequence, the sum of two consecutive terms gives the next term. [True/False]

Answer Sheet

1) T, 2) F, 3) T, 4) T, 5) T, 6) T, 7) F, 8) F, 9) T, 10) T

Short Answer

1. What is the value of the golden ratio?

2. Which symbol do we use to express the golden ratio?

3. What is the name of the mathematician who first introduced the golden ratio?

4. What is equal to the sum of two adjacent Fibonacci terms?

5. What number do the ratios of two adjacent Fibonacci terms approach as the number of terms increases?

Answer Sheet

1. 1.618

2. Letter Φ (phi).

3. Euclid

4. The next term

5. The golden ratio

Multiple–Choice Questions

1. What is the number 1.618033988749895… called?

a. Golden ratio.

b. Gravitational acceleration

c. Density of the air

d. Euler constant.

2. What is the first Fibonacci term?

a. 1

b. 2

c. 3

d. 5

3. Which of the following is the name of the mathematician who first introduced the golden ratio?

a. Pythagoras

b. Euclid

c. Plato

d. Petron

4. Here are some terms of the Fibonacci sequence 1 1 2 3 5 8 13 21 34 ... What is the next term in the Fibonacci sequence?

a. 45

b. 55

c. 67

d. 47

5. Look at the photo below. What do we call that division?

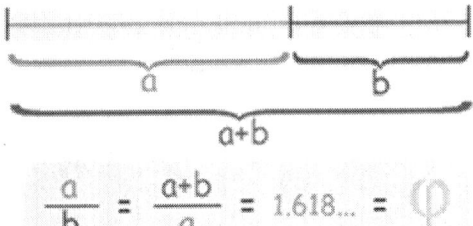

a. Equivalent distribution

b. Euclidean division

c. Extreme and mean division

d. Fibonacci distribution

6. Which of the following is false?

a. The golden ratio is the number 1.618.

b. The mathematician who first introduced the golden ratio was Euclid.

c. The ratio of two successive Fibonacci terms gives the golden ratio.

d. The second term in the Fibonacci sequence is 2.

7. What is the sum of the first five Fibonacci numbers?

a. 10

b. 11

c. 12

d. 13

8. What would be the number of petals in the plant in the next turn?

a. 18

b. 19

c. 20

d. 21

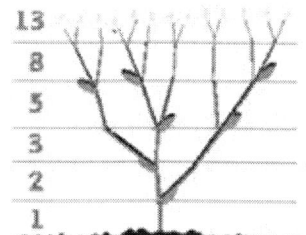

9. What is the symbol that we use to show the golden ratio?

a. Φ

b. €

c. Ω

d. μ

10. What is the sum of the tenth and 12th terms in the Fibonacci sequence?

a. 196

b. 197

c. 198

d. 199

11. We know about a sequence that $x_1 = 1$, $x_2 = 1$, and $x_{n+1} = x_n + x_n - 1$. What is the 15th term of that sequence?

a. 608

b. 609

c. 610

d. 611

12. If I multiply each term in the Fibonacci sequence by two, what would be the fifth term?

a. 10

b. 11

c. 12

d. 13

13. What is the difference between the sixth term and the fourth term in the Fibonacci sequence?

a. 4

b. 5

c. 6

d. 7

14. What is the sum of the second five terms of the Fibonacci sequence?

a. 100

b. 120

c. 110

d. 150

15. What is the sum of the first two Fibonacci terms that have two digits?

a. 23

b. 32

c. 34

d. 43

Answer Sheet

1) A, 2) A, 3) B, 4) B, 5) C, 6) D, 7) C, 8) D, 9) A, 10) D, 11) C, 12) A, 13) B, 14) C, 15) C

ALTERNATIVE ASSESSMENT

Task 1: Exploring the Golden Ratio in Pine Cones

The teacher assigns the students to find at least three different pine cones and count the seeds in both directions starting from the center. The students are expected to explore the Fibonacci terms that appear in the number of seeds in the pine cones. The students are required to answer the question of how the golden ratio appears in the pine cones. In other words, students are required to link the number of seeds to the golden ratio by first exploring the Fibonacci terms. The teacher suggests the strategy of coloring the spirals in the pine cones to count them easily, a method that is also mentioned in the explanation part. The students are asked to visit the web site located at http://www.homeschoolmath.net/teaching/fibonacci_golden_section.php

Rubric 1: Exploring the Golden Ratio in Pine Cones

	Understanding the problem	**Planning a solution**	**Getting an answer**
4–3	The problem is totally understood, the student calculates the number of seeds in the pine cones and relates it to the golden ratio.	The student uses the linked sample to handle the problem and uses the sample as a benchmark for counting the other pine cones.	The seeds in the pine cones are counted correctly and linked to the Fibonacci sequence and hence to the golden ratio.
2–1	The problem is not fully understood, the seeds in the pine cones are either calculated incorrectly or not calculated at all, or there is no linking of the findings to the golden ratio.	The given sample is not analyzed properly, leading to an either erroneous or incomplete strategy for counting the number of seeds.	The calculation of the number of seeds is incorrect or incomplete or there are errors in linking it to the Fibonacci sequence and the golden ratio.
0	The problem is totally misunderstood, or the study gives no information showing an understanding of the problem.	The given sample is not analyzed in relation to other samples found by the student, or there is no strategy for handling the problem.	There is no calculation of the number of seeds or no link to the Fibonacci sequence and the golden ratio.

Task 2: Graphing the Fibonacci Sequence and Calculating the Ratios

The teacher asks the students to construct a graph in which the x–axis shows the first 20 terms, and the y–axis shows the ratios of consecutive terms. That is, the x–coordinates of the points come from the Fibonacci terms, and the y–coordinates come from the ratios of the terms used to form the x–coordinate and the previous Fibonacci terms. The students are asked to plot the points on the graph and then observe and express what number those ratios approach.

You can use Utah State University's software to calculate the ratios between consecutive Fibonacci terms.

Rubric 2: Graphing the Fibonacci Sequence and Calculating the Ratios

	Understanding the problem	Planning a solution	Getting an answer
4–3	The problem is fully understood, and links between the Fibonacci terms and the golden ratio are correctly interpreted.	The student uses the given software efficiently to calculate the ratios, and a planned strategy can be observed and understood.	The calculations are error-free, the plotting of the points on the graph is correct, and the number the ratios of consecutive terms approach is correctly determined.
2–1	The problem is not fully understood or is misunderstood, or the link between the Fibonacci sequence and the golden ratio is not correctly interpreted.	The suggested software is not used to analyze the problem.	Errors occur in the calculation of the ratios, there is fallacious plotting of the points on the line, or the term that the ratios approach cannot be determined.
0	The problem is totally misunderstood, or the study gives no information showing an understanding of the problem.	The given sample is not used to calculate the ratios, or there is no sign of a strategy being used.	There is no calculation of the ratios or no plotting of the terms on the coordinate axes.

Task 3: Exploring the Golden Ratio in the Human Body

The teacher asks the students to investigate in what parts of the human body the golden ratio is observed. Students are expected to state at least three parts of the human body in which the golden ratio appears and how it appears. In addition, students are expected to write a short article and make a short presentation about their findings and their understanding of their research. Further, the teacher asks the students to give their references.

Rubric 3: Exploring Golden Ratio in Human Body

	Research	**Article**	**Presentation**
4–3	Research is done through appropriate sources, terms are understood, and several sources are used.	Information is presented properly, content is handled properly, at least three places where the golden ratio appears are mentioned, and ideas are suitably presented in good language.	The presentation involves visual tools, and the key ideas are highlighted.
2–1	Only a very little research is conducted, the sources include non-reliable data, or terms are misunderstood.	Transfer of information in the text seems sloppy, content is not handled carefully, fewer than three topics are investigated, or the language is used poorly.	Key points are not emphasized, or visual tools are used minimally or improperly.
0	There is no research or no sign of even attempting to conduct the study.	Either no article or a very imprecise text full of wrong ideas is used.	There is either no presentation or a sloppy presentation of the study.

Rubric 4 (Extension activity)

	Interpreting the shapes of spirals
4	An excellent explanation of the reason for the shape is given, ideas are strongly linked to the Fibonacci sequence, and the golden ratio and associated ideas are supported with skillful rationales.
3	The explanation of the situation is good, ideas are properly linked to the Fibonacci sequence and the golden ratio, and nearly perfect rationales to support the stated ideas are included.
2	The explanation of the ideas to link them to the Fibonacci sequence includes some reasonable parts but also has missing parts, and ideas are insufficiently supported by the rationales.
1	The explanation of the shapes of spirals is sloppy, many unreasonable ideas are included, or few or no rationales are given to support the ideas.
0	Very little or no effort to explain the reasons for the shape is exerted, or no rationales at all are given.

AUTHOR

Osman Canavar

Primary Education Department

Boğaziçi University

3 ARCHIMEDES' PRINCIPLE: BUOYANCY FORCE

INTRODUCTION

There are many objects of various sizes and attributes that populate or fill aquatic environments. Some of these objects are living organisms, such as fish, algae, or humans while others are non–living, such as rocks, sand, or ships. Some live at a sea, lake or river, and others just use them. Some objects prefer the bottom of the sea, while others like the surface. In addition, scientists inspired by the floating of a piece of wood on water designed small boats and then giant, heavy ships. What are the factors that affect objects in liquids? Is it possible that heavy objects are raised more easily in the water rather than in the air? This lesson will talk about these issues and try to connect real–life skills to interdisciplinary areas.

OBJECTIVES

Mathematics

– Students are expected to compare and order two or more objects according to weight/mass.

– Students are expected to use addition and subtraction to solve problems.

– Students are expected to use tables and symbols to represent and describe proportional and other relationships.

– Students are expected to measure volume by using measurement tools.

Science

– Students are expected to compare weight of an object in air and liquid.

– Students are expected to realize that there is a upwards force applied on an object by liquid, buoyancy force.

– Students are expected to identify factors that contribute to how objects move in a liquid.

Technology

– Students are expected to use technology in self–directed activities.

– Students are expected to use software programs with audio, video, and graphics to enhance learning experiences.

Engineering

– Students are expected to use rational thinking to develop or improve a product

– Students are expected to use an engineering notebook to record the final design, construction, and manipulation of finished projects

MATERIALS

– Computer for each student

– A projector

– Internet access

STUDENT INTRODUCTION

The teacher asks the students whether they have ever heard of Archimedes. Most probably, many students have heard of him, but the students may not know of his principles, research, or discoveries. The teacher begins to tell Archimedes' story. About 2000 years ago, King II Hieron had an imperial crown made, but then wondered whether the jeweler had substituted silver inside the gold crown, so he asked Archimedes to determine this. Archimedes began to work on this issue, but could not find an answer. One day, Archimedes went to the bath and felt that his weight decreased. He hypothesized that the amount of water removed was related to the volume of the body inside the water and immediately left the bath. What had he discovered? What is the relation between the water removed and the object that sinks in the water? Answering these questions made Archimedes one of the most prominent scientists in the world.

ENGAGEMENT

The teacher begins the lesson by showing a video related to scuba diving located at the following web site:

http://www.youtube.com/watch?v=ruUdvXHmoC0&feature=related

After the students watch the video, the teacher asks about the important factors that affect divers, what impact these factors have on buoyancy, and what a diver needs to know to control buoyancy. Then, they begin to discuss these issues.

EXPLORATION

The teacher divides the students into two groups and asks them to use simulations. Each group is asked to record factors that affect the buoyancy of an object. These simulations are directly related to buoyancy and can be accessed at

http://phet.colorado.edu/en/simulation/buoyancy.

The aim of this activity is to get students to engage in thinking about how objects sink or float, not to foster students' understanding of the concept. It is only expected that students work on the simulations; they manipulate the objects and observe the results. The first group records what happens, if blocks are same mass, volume, and density. They are expected to write the values of the block in a table and briefly explain each condition. The second group makes a graph according to changes in the buoyancy simulation.

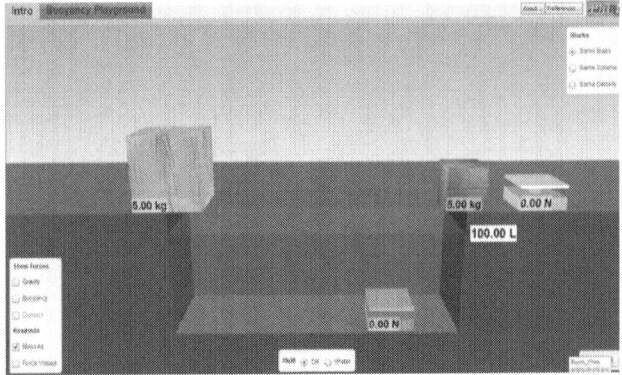

Figure 1.

EXPLANATION

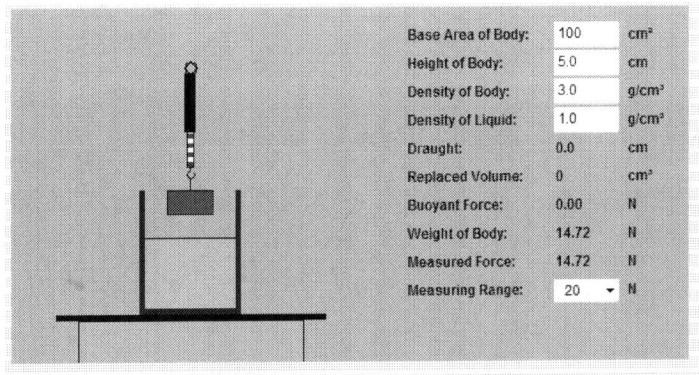

Figure 2.

When the students use the simulations, they only record the results. They make observations about the factors that affect the buoyancy. Then, the teacher asks why it is that a small stone sinks in water but big ships float on water. Now, the teacher explains the concept of buoyancy described above and illustrates the simulation by changing values in the white areas. Then, the teacher gives the formula for the buoyancy force and weight of the object in a liquid.

Buoyancy force = Weight of the object in air − Weight of the object in liquid

Next, the teacher asks the students to discuss the differences among these three pictures.

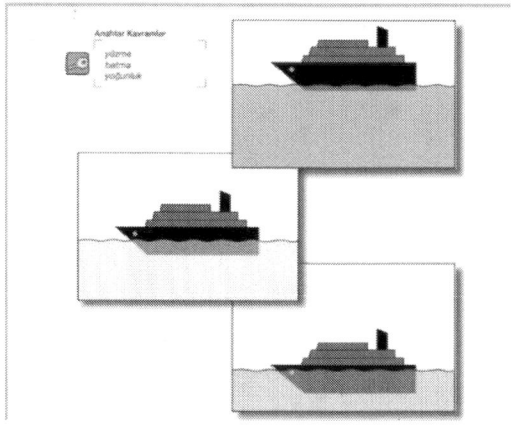

Figure 3.

The teacher provides more details about sinking and floating. The buoyancy force is related to the immersed volume of the object, the density of the liquid, and gravity. Why are the volumes of these ships in liquids different? It is because the densities of liquids are not the same. The density of the liquid and the immersed volume of the object are directly proportional to the buoyancy force. Moreover, the volume and depth of the liquid do not have any influence on the buoyancy force. In addition, the position of the object in the liquid is related to the density of the both the object and the liquid.

– The density of the liquid = The density of the object:

    The object remains stationary.

–The density of the liquid > The density of the object:

    The object floats.

–The density of the liquid < The density of the object:

    The object sinks.

Then, the teacher gives a demonstration of the movement of a ball in liquid. http://demonstrations.wolfram.com/FloatingBall

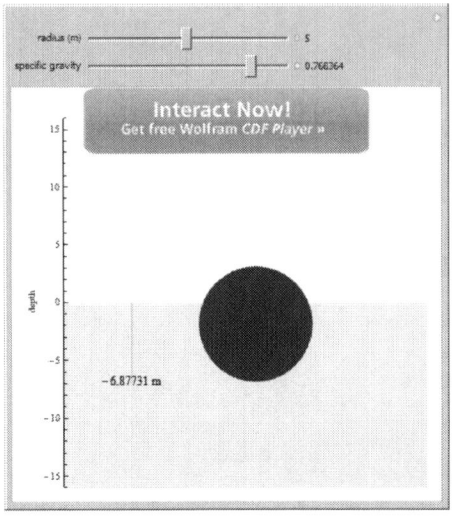

Figure 4.

EXTENSION

The teacher asks for a formula for the buoyancy force. The students know the relationship between the density of the liquid and the immersed volume of the object. Then, the teacher guides the students to figure out the formula.

EVALUATION

True and False

Circle the correct answer

1. The weight of a stone in water is lighter than the weight of the stone in air. [True/False]

2. Liquids apply the same buoyancy force to all objects. [True/False]

3. The buoyancy force is an upward force. [True/False]

4. As the volume of the object inside the liquid increases the buoyancy force increases. [True/False]

5. Lighter objects float, while heavier objects sink. [True/False]

6. The buoyancy force is related to the density of the liquid. [True/False]

7. The buoyancy force is related to the density of the object. [True/False]

8. The buoyancy force is equal to the volume of the displaced liquid. [True/False]

9. Objects sink in water when they have greater mass than water. [True/False]

10. The depth and height of the water do not affect the position of the ships. [True/False]

Answer Sheet

1) T, 2) F, 3) T, 4) T, 5) F, 6) T, 7) F, 8) T, 9) F, 10) T

Short Answer

1) Explain how a shark swims based on the given information and using the given words. (Buoyancy force, density of the liquid or object)

2) Explain the following statement briefly: "Sharks lack bones that help fish to swim, but have a swim bladder. The amount of gas in the swim bladder

changes when a fish moves up or down or remains stationary in the water. However, sharks have huge livers that contain oil." The density of a scuba diver is important for floating or sinking. A diver decreases or increases his or her density by using a buoyancy compensator.

3) How does the buoyancy force have an impact on the weight of the object in the water?

4) Briefly explain the relationship between the volume of the object and the buoyancy force.

5) How does the density of a liquid affect the volume of the object in the liquid?

6) What is the relationship between the density of the liquid and that of the object?

Answer Sheet

1) Air and oil are less dense than water. This is necessary for floating on water. The buoyancy force exerted on the shark is related to the density of the water, and a shark has oil in its liver, so the density of the shark becomes less than the water, and the shark swims in the water.

2) If the diver wants to sink in the water, the diver increases his or her own density. Otherwise, the diver decreases his or her own density to float in the water. For this purpose, a buoyancy compensator is used.

3) The buoyancy force pushes the object upward against the gravity force, which is downward. The net force is equal to the difference of buoyancy and gravity, so the weight of the object in water is less than in air.

4) The buoyancy force is related to the volume of the object in the

liquid. As the volume of the object is immersed more in liquid, the buoyancy force also increases.

5) As the density of the liquid increases, the buoyancy force also increases. Thus, the immersed volume decreases and the object rises.

6) The density of the liquid = The density of the object: The object remains stationary in mid water.

The density of the liquid > The density of the object: The object floats.

The density of the liquid < The density of the object: The object sinks.

Multiple–Choice Questions

1. The buoyancy force increases if

a. the volume of the object in the water increases.

b. the density of the object increases.

c. the volume of the liquid increases.

d. the mass of the liquid increases.

2. If the density of the liquid increases, the object

a. sinks in the liquid.

b. floats on the surface of the liquid.

c. remains stationary in the liquid.

d. rises a little.

3. If the density of the object increases, the object

a. sinks in the liquid.

b. floats on the surface of the liquid.

c. remains stationary.

d. rises a little.

4. If the densities of the liquid and the object are equal, then the object

a. moves horizontally.

b. sinks.

c. rises.

d. remains stationary.

5) An object is immersed in water, and the level of the water rises. Thus, the displaced water equals

a. the mass of the object.

b. the volume of the object.

c. the mass of the liquid.

6) The buoyancy force equals

a. the volume of the object.

b. the mass of the object.

c. the mass of the liquid.

d. the displaced volume of the liquid.

7) If a scuba diver wants to sink in water, the diver should not

a. increase his or her own density.

b. decrease his or her own density.

c. carry heavier weights.

8) Which of the following does not affect the buoyancy force.

a. Gravity

b. The density of the liquid

c. The volume of the object

d. The volume of the object in the liquid

9) If object X is immersed into diverse liquids, which of these inequalities is true?

 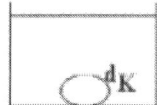  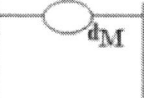

a. $d_K > d_L$

b. $d_L > d_M$

c. $d_X < d_M$

d. $d_X < d_L$

10) All of the objects remain stationary. What is the relationship among the densities of the objects?

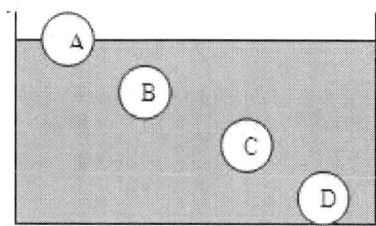

a. $A < B < C < D$ 	 b. $A > B > C > D$

c. $A < B = C < D$ 	 d. $A > B = C > D$

11) If the objects are balanced, which of these statements is true?

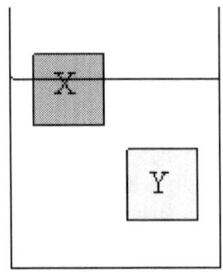

a. $d_X > d_{liquid}$

b. $d_{liquid} = d_Y > d_X$

c. $d_Y > d_{liquid}$

d. $d_X = d_{liquid} < d_Y$

12) If the weight of an object in air is 32N, and the buoyancy force is 8N, then what is the weight of the object in the liquid?

a. 18

b. 8

c. 24

d. 20

Answer Sheet

1) A, 2) B, 3) A, 4) D, 5) D, 6) D, 7) B, 8) C, 9) C, 10) C, 11) B, 12) C

ALTERNATIVE ASSESSMENT

The students are divided into three groups. Each group is expected to design a sea transport using Archimedes' Principle. The first ship floats on water, the second remains stationary, and the last sinks. The students can use any material they need for the project.

Task 1

The students are asked to record all measurements, designs, drawings, and calculations.

Rubric 1: Engineering Notebook

	Measurements of the transport	**Drawings**	**Calculations**
4–3	The length, width, volume, mass, and heights are measured.	The project is drawn in full detail.	All calculations related to the buoyancy force, the density of the liquid and object, and the volume of the object are performed.
2–1	One of the measurements is missing.	The project is only partially drawn.	One of the calculations is missing.
0	There is no measurement.	There is no drawing.	There is no calculation.

Task 2

Students are asked to write what happened during the preparation of the project, and how they feel and interact with the group members.

Rubric 2: Engineering Notebook

	Difficulties	Ease	Interactions with group peers
4–3	The students mention all difficulties that they encounter. These include technical difficulties, theoretical difficulties, individual difficulties, and the like.	The students mention all ease that they experienced. This includes the benefits of working as a group instead of individually, collaboration, and the like.	The setting and communication among the group members is good.
2–1	One or two difficulties are mentioned.	Only briefly information about the ease is provided.	There are communication gaps.
0	No information about the difficulties is provided.	No information is provided.	There is no communication.

Task 3

Students are asked to make a model for each project.

Rubric 3: Project Model

	Appearance	Solidity	Validity
4–3	The student uses imaginative appearance, colors, and materials.	The model is rigid and resists staying in the water.	The model is appropriate to the aim and works successfully.
2–1	The appearance is not imaginative.	The model is not resistant.	The model is partially appropriate to the aim.
0	There is no imagination.	The model is weak.	The model is not appropriate.

AUTHOR

Gizem Yeter Bas

Primary Education Department

Boğaziçi University

4 SOUND

INTRODUCTION

Sound Waves, Properties of Sound Waves

Sound is very important, primarily in communication, as many of us might guess. In addition, sound is essential for many purposes in ocean exploration, hunting, underground resources, health, and the like. Sound is produced by a source in the form of waves. We can think of sound waves as being like water waves in terms of how they propagate and most other properties as well, in order to make it more concrete in our minds. On the other hand, unlike water waves, sound waves can propagate also in gases and solids. It is possible to manipulate some characteristics of sound waves, such as amplitude, wavelength, frequency, and speed.

The aim of this project is to provide an awareness of this reality that surrounds us and also to guide the students through an exploration of new useful tools. In this project, the students will first identify some properties of waves to learn how sound waves look and how to manipulate them. Then, some factors affecting the speed of sound waves will be examined through some classroom activities. The students will compare sound speed in different media by making observations. In order to foster students' understanding and to facilitate their learning, knowledge from interdisciplinary areas in STEM education, such as mathematics and engineering, will be drawn on.

OBJECTIVES

Mathematics

– Students are expected to know linearly and inverse proportion.

– Students are expected to define sinus wave to recognize the amplitude of sound wave.

– Students are expected to state frequency as 1/period which are mathematical terms.

– Students are expected to relate the formula of speed in mathematics which is distance/time with speed of sound waves which is frequency×wavelength

Science

– Students are expected to identify and describe the characteristics of amplitude, wavelength, frequency and pitch for a sound wave.

– Students are expected to identify factors effecting (and not effecting) the speed of a sound wave.

– Students are expected to rank liquid, solid and gas media according to the speed with which a wave propagates through it.

Technology

– Students are expected to state uses of ultrasound in some engineering like biomedical engineering, mining engineering etc.

MATERIALS

– Computer

– An LCD projector

– Ruler, clamp and wooden wedges

– Shoe box

– Stapler

– Water glasses (~6)

– Water pitcher

– Various objects of different mediums (eg: wooden block, metal pipe, book)

– Tuning fork

STUDENT INTRODUCTION

Technological inventions are created regularly in the world. They facilitate our lives in many fields. In today's world, there are many devices that were invented using properties of sound. Ultrasound is one of them. When you have gone to a hospital, has the doctor sent you for an ultrasound? Do you know the function of ultrasound in medicine? Have you ever wondered about why it is called ultrasound? What kind of relationship could it have with sound? What are some other devices based on sound?

As young researchers, you are assigned to give brief explanations to these questions. To be able to answer these questions, you must have enough necessary information about sound. You must also learn some basic terms about sound with their meanings. To facilitate your learning, you will watch some related videos and animations. You will also engage in fun and useful activities.

ENGAGEMENT

The teacher starts the lesson with an interesting question to attract the students' attraction. "Is there anybody who doesn't know about the Mexican Wave or stadium wave?" For students who do not know it, the teacher shows a video illustrating how the Mexican Wave is performed with funny music. The video is available at the web site located at

http://www.acoustics.salford.ac.uk/schools/lesson1/flash/mexicanwave.swf

.Then the teacher chooses about ten students and arranges them in a circle about one arm's length apart. He or she asks the students to perform a Mexican Wave as in in the video. While the progression of the wave continues, the teacher points out that although the wave is moving around the circle, the students themselves are not moving, other than to lift up their arms. He or she says that we hear a vibrating wave of air molecule waves as sound, and sound waves work like this. Then the teacher shows another animation that includes the motion of vibrating air molecules from the web site located at.

http://www.cabrillo.edu/~jmccullough/Applets/Flash/Fluids,%20Oscillations%20and%20Waves/PressureDisplacement.swf.

The aim is to enable students to see the relationship between the Mexican Wave and sound waves, while motivating them into the lesson. Then, the teacher asks students to draw the transmission of sound with air particles in their journals as they watch in video. In addition, he or she asks students to complete the K column (What do I know?) of a KWL chart based on their previous knowledge about waves. This part of the project lasts about one hour.

EXPLORATION

The teacher divides the students into homogenous groups. He or she says, "Each of you is a researcher, and you are trying to design a musical instrument. With this goal in mind, you search relationships among properties of a vibrating object with attention to the height and the amount of stress. You will observe this with ruler activity." Then he or she gives the students rulers, clamps, and wooden wedges. The teacher asks the students to pose their own hypotheses and to write them in their journals and then distributes rubrics to students to evaluate their friends' performances. Next, he or she gives directions. The students are told to hold the ruler partially off the edge of a table or desk and then press down and release the end of the ruler that is off the desk. Their aim is to try to produce different sounds by varying the length of the part of the ruler that is off the desk. After the students finish their observations, the teacher asks them to fill in their worksheets and present them (Attachment 1). Then, he or she gives two questions to investigate until the next meeting and to write in the W columns (What do I want to know?) of their journals. The two questions are

– As a musical instrument designer, what should you do to produce different sounds?

– Why do individual sounds differ from each other?

(This part of the project lasts about one hour.)

EXPLANATION

In the first part of this project, students learned that a wave is a moving disturbance in a medium such as air, a solid, or a liquid. Now, key terms such as crest (compression) and trough (rarefaction) are covered in order to understand the structure of a wave. It is stated that a crest is the greatest disturbance point of a wave, while a trough is the lowest. The propagation of sound waves is explained in terms of a "golf ball–spring model" with the aim of making it concrete in students' minds. This model consists of golf balls connected by springs. The golf balls represent molecules, and the springs represent forces between molecules. The first ball is pushed toward the next one and compresses the spring. The compressed spring pushes the next adjacent ball, and so on. The disturbance caused by moving the first ball takes some time to travel to the last one. Compression in a spring applies a force to the previous golf ball. In returning to its initial position, the spring expands. In a real propagation medium, a disturbance consists of a compression followed by a rarefaction that allows the medium to return to its normal state (see Figure 1). The direction of a disturbance's travel with crests and troughs is shown in a sinusoidal graph to make it easy to describe and to determine some characteristics of sound waves (see Figures 2 and 3).

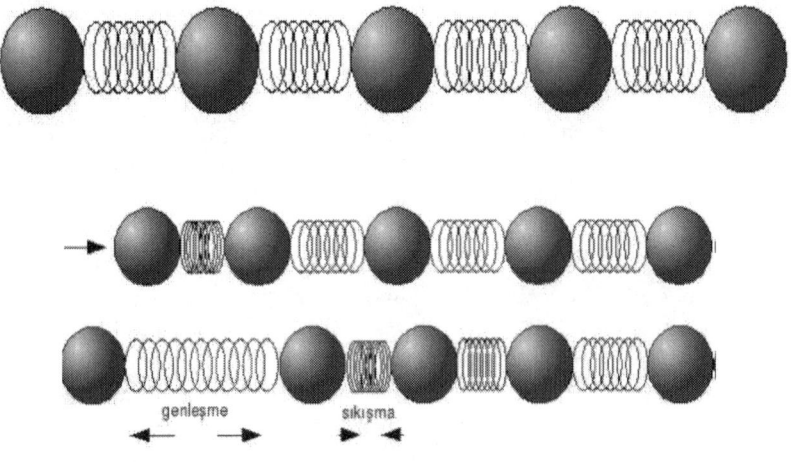

Figure 1

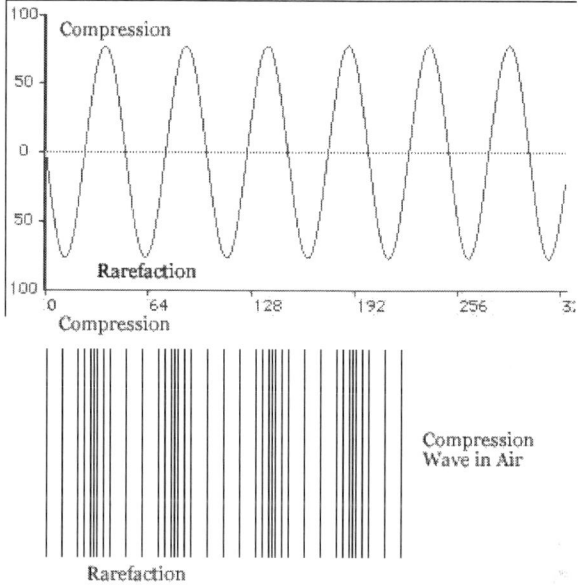

Figure 2

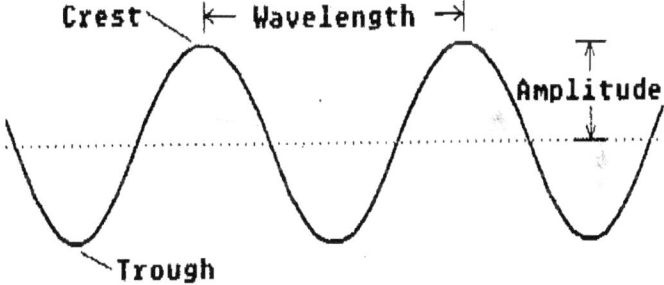

Figure 3

Then the teacher guides the students to learn some properties of sound waves such as amplitude, wavelength, frequency, and pitch. He or she draws a graph like Figure 3 onto the board to explain these terms. The wavelength is defined as the distance between two adjacent crests or troughs of a wave. The amplitude is half of the vertical distance between one crest and the next trough. The amplitude of a sound determines its volume. That is, larger amplitudes create louder sounds than smaller ones. The frequency of a sound is the number of waves that pass a point each second. It is measured in Hertz. The teacher gives an example to make it understandable, such as that if 50 waves pass through a given point in 10 seconds, the frequency is $50/10 = 5$. It is recalled that the period is the time it takes to complete a wave, a fact that students know from their study of mathematics. Then, it is emphasized that the frequency is the inverse of this, that is, the number of cycles in a second. This means that frequency = 1/period. The pitch represents the perceived fundamental frequency of a sound. A sound with a high frequency has a high pitch, while a sound with a low frequency has a low pitch. For instance, a bird makes a low–pitched sound, and a lion makes a high–pitched sound. Then, the teacher assigns a quiz to check the students' learning.

The second part of the project consists of three activities that review previous learning and also introduce new information about sound. The aim of these activities is to observe factors influencing sound and the various properties of sound waves. The teacher divides the students into three groups. He or she puts the necessary materials for each activity into tables with worksheets (Attachment 2). After explaining the activities to the students, he or she gives them 15 minutes to complete it. At the end, the teacher asks the students to present their results.

In the third part of project, the teacher asks the students to guess whether sound or light travels at a higher speed. He or she gives thunder as a hint. Then, the students are asked to predict in which state of matter sound travels fastest and what the reasons could be. In addition, he or she asks what factors affect the speed of sound based on previous learning. The students are asked to write them into the K, W, and L columns of their journals. For ten minutes, they discuss these questions in the classroom. Then, the teacher guides the students in studying the speed of sound. The speed of sound is defined as how fast the disturbance passes from particle to particle. The general formula for speed is recalled, namely, speed = distance/time. For the speed of sound, the faster a sound wave travels, the more distance it will cover in the same period of time.

Then, an example problem is solved on the board. For instance, if a sound wave is observed to travel a distance of 500 meter in two seconds, the speed of the sound wave is 500/2 = 250 m/s. Students are warned not to confuse the meanings of speed and frequency. It should be emphasized that frequency refers to "how often?", while speed refers to "how fast?" Then, the formula for sound waves is given. Since the relationship between frequency and period (time) has already been learned, the mathematical expression of sound is given by the formula speed = wavelength × frequency. After recalling all this, the teacher compares and explains the speed of sound in different media. He or she states that if particles of matter are closely spaced, the speed of sound is faster. In addition, the degree of tightness of connected particles affects the speed of sound. Thus, the speed of sound occurs in the order solids > liquids > gases. The main points and formulas are written on the board and into notebooks.

Then, an interesting video with 15 minutes about sound is watched from the web site located at http://www.youtube.com/watch?v=6f0hsbFHYvs.

The students discuss what they understand from the video for five minutes. After the video, some applications are performed on the animation. The complete summary of leaning about sound is on the web site located at http://www.educationscotland.gov.uk/resources/s/sound/solid.asp?strRefer ringChannel=resources&strReferringPageID=tcm:4–248295–64. These fun applications help the students to review what they have learned, especially the visual learners. In these applications, variables can be changed, as shown in the example photos. This helps students to make clear observations.

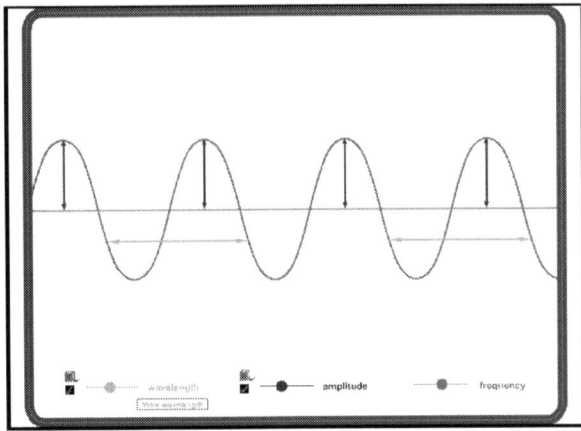

Figure 4

EXTENSION

In this part of the project, students are assigned to search for usage areas of ultrasound, after its properties are mentioned in the classroom.

EVALUATION

True and False

Circle the correct answer

1. If a sound becomes louder, the frequency of the sound wave is likely increasing. [True/False]

2. Sound can travel in a vacuum. [True/False]

3. If the frequency of a sound is doubled, its speed is also doubled. [True/False]

4. The formula for the speed of wave is speed = amplitude × frequency. [True/False]

5. The amplitude of sound determines the volume of sound. [True/False]

6. The frequency of sound affects its speed. [True/False]

7. Wavelength is the number of complete waves that pass a point in one second. [True/False]

8. If a vibrator strikes water ten times in one second, then the frequency of the wave is five. [True/False]

9. Sound with a high frequency has a high pitch. [True/False]

10. The degree of tightness of connected particles affects the speed of sound. [True/False]

Answer Sheet

1) T, 2) F, 3) F, 4) F, 5) T, 6) F, 7) F, 8) F, 9) T, 10) T

Short Answer

1. Define the frequency of a sound wave.

2. An elephant produces a 10 Hz sound wave. Assuming the speed of sound in air is 345 m/s, determine the wavelength of this infrasonic sound wave.

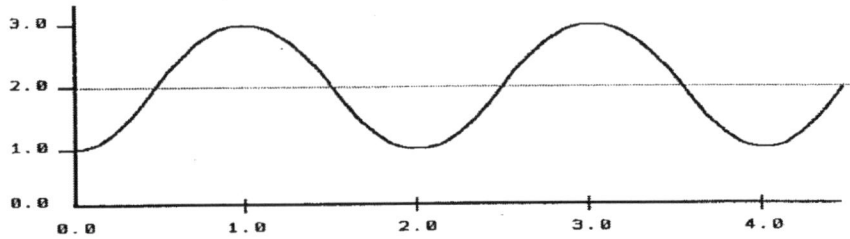

3. Find the number of crests and troughs of the wave.

4. Find the wavelength and amplitude of the wave.

5. Calculate the speed of a sound wave travelling 30 meters in 10 seconds.

Answer Sheet

1. Frequency is the number of complete waves that pass a point in one second.

2. speed = wavelength × frequency

345 = wavelength × 10   345/10 = 34.5 m

3. three troughs and two crests

4. wavelength = 3 − 1 = 2 cm   amplitude = 2 − 1 = 1 cm

5. speed = distance/time; speed = 30/10 = 3 m/s

Multiple–Choice Questions

1) The relationship between speed, velocity, and wavelength is

a) wavelength = speed × frequency

b) frequency = speed × wavelength

c) speed = wavelength × frequency

d) wavelength = frequency/speed

2) The frequency of a wave travelling at a speed of 100 ms is 20 Hz. Its period will be _____.

a) 0.05   b) 0.04   c) 20   d) 25

3) The amplitude of a wave is _____.

a) the distance the wave moves in one second

b) the distance the wave moves in one period of the wave

c) the maximum distance moved by the medium particles on either side of the mean position

d) the distance equal to one wave length

4) Sound waves don't travel in

a) solids.

b) liquids.

c) a vacuum.

d) gases.

5) If 100 waves pass through a given point in 10 seconds, the frequency is found to be

a) 4   b) 5   c) 8   d) 10

6) The main factor affecting the speed of a sound wave is the _____.

a) amplitude of the sound wave

b) intensity of the sound wave

c) loudness of the sound wave

d) properties of the medium

7) Which one of the following factors determines the pitch of a sound?

a) the amplitude of the sound wave

b) the distance of the sound wave from the source

c) the frequency of the sound wave

d) the phases of different parts of the sound wave

8) A vibrating object with a frequency of 200 Hz produces sound that travels through air at 360 m/s. The number of meters separating the adjacent compressions in the sound wave is _____.

a) 0.90

b) 1.8

c) 3.6

d) 7.2

9) What is the appropriate order of these three waves from the lowest pitch to the highest?

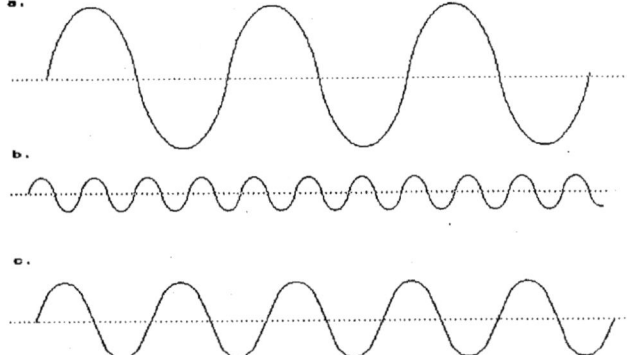

a) b > a > c   b) a > b > c   c) c > b > a   d) b > c > a

10) A sound source produces waves of 400 Hz and wavelength 2.5 m. The speed of the sound waves is

a) 100 m/s

b) 1,000 m/s

c) 10,000 m/s

d) 3,000 km/s

Answer Sheet

1) C, 2) A, 3) C, 4) C, 5) D, 6) D, 7) C, 8) B, 9) D, 10) B

ALTERNATIVE ASSESSMENT

Task 1. SOUNDS ARE VIBRATING…

How do the length and stress of a ruler affect its sound?

Materials

– ruler with length 30 cm

– clamp

– wooden blocks

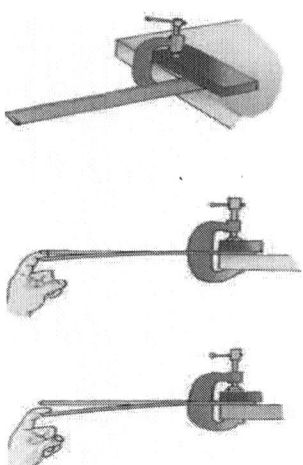

Procedure:

1) Try to produce different sounds by varying the length of a ruler.

2) Set up two hypotheses and test them.

Hypothesis 1	Hypothesis 2
Variables?	Variables?

Let us Discuss:

1) Discuss the correctness of your hypotheses.

2) Think about what other factors might be affecting the sound of a vibrated ruler.

Rubric 1: Investigating Sound Vibrations

Categories	Satisfactory	Needs improvement	Unsatisfactory
	10–6	6–3	3–1
Variables	The variables are clearly defined.	The variables are not clearly defined.	There are no variables.
Hypotheses	The hypotheses are reasonable and are substantiated by the activity.	The hypotheses are substantially reasonable.	The hypotheses are not complete or do not flow logically from the research.
Group Working	There is good collaboration between group members. Every member generates new ideas.	Only some of the group members do any work.	There is no collaboration.
Discussion and Presentation	Factors are clearly defined, and different alternative factors are found.	Factors are clearly defined.	Factors are not found.
Assignment	Logical answers are given, and different sources are used.	Logical answers are given.	The answers given are irrelevant.
Total	.		

Task 2. SOUND WAVES

Purpose: To facilitate students' understanding of sound waves, including their properties and behaviors

Materials:

– Shoe box

– Rubber bands

– Stapler

– Water glasses (~6)

– Water pitcher

– Various objects of different media (e.g., wooden block, metal pipe, book)

– Tuning fork

Activity 1:

On the desk are various objects, a glass of water, and a tuning fork. What do you think will happen to the sound you hear from the tuning fork, when you place it in contact with the following objects?

Wooden block:

Metal pipe:

Book:

Now test your hypotheses. Tap the tuning fork lightly on the desk and press it against each object. Record your observations.

Wooden block:

Metal Pipe:

Book:

What is causing the differences?

Now tap the tuning fork on the desk and place it in the water. Record your observations. Use the keywords: wavelength, amplitude, and frequency.

What is the relationship between what you heard or maybe felt with the various objects and what you saw in the water?

Activity 2:

On the desk you will see a shoe box and several rubber bands. Your task is to create four different sounds using the rubber bands. These sounds are called pitch. Staple each rubber band to a different end of the shoe box.

What do you think will produce different pitches?

Test your hypothesis.

How did you make each rubber band produce a different pitch?

What caused a higher pitch?

What caused a lower pitch? Can you make the lower pitch sound louder than the higher pitch?

When you pluck the rubber bands, what do you notice about the box and the rubber bands? Use the keywords: pitch, vibration, frequency, and speed.

You have just created your own guitar! What you experience happening here is similar to what happens when you pluck guitar strings! The mechanical waves create vibrations that move through a medium from one location to another. This is similar to what happens in your ear!

Activity 3:

On the desk is a pitcher of water, a spoon, and several drinking glasses. Your task is to create different sounds from each glass using the water and the spoon. The sound produced has a property called pitch.

What do you think will create different pitches?

Test out your hypothesis.

How did you create the different pitches?

What made a higher pitch? Is the higher pitch louder?

What made a lower pitch? Is the lower pitch softer?

Why do you think those things made different pitches? Use the keywords: pitch, air molecules, and frequency.

Rubric 2: Properties of Sound Waves

CATEGORY	Beginning 1	Developing 2	Accomplished 3	Well Accomplished 4
Research and Gather Information	The student does not collect any information that relates to the topic.	The student collects very little information, or only some of it relates to the topic.	The student collects some basic information, and most of it relates to the topic.	The student collects a great deal of information, and all of it relates to the topic.
Share Information	The student does not share any information.	The student shares either too little information or irrelevant information	The student shares some information, some of which is relevant	The student shares a lot of information that is relevant to the topic.
Fulfill Team Role's Duties	The student relies on others to do the work or does not perform the assigned team role.	The student rarely does the assigned work, needs many reminders, or does not perform the assigned team role.	The student rarely needs reminding to complete the work and usually performs the assigned team role.	The student always does the assigned work without being reminded and performs the assigned team role.
Participation	The student does not speak during the activity.	The student either helps too little or says things that are irrelevant to the topic.	The student offers some information that is mostly relevant	The student participates actively by helping and providing relevant information
Attitudes to others	The student usually wants his or her own view considered, while ignoring other views.	The student often sides with friends instead of considering all views.	The student sometimes considers all views to come to a fair solution.	The student considers all views to come to a fair solution.
TOTAL				

Rubric 3: Extension Assignment

Category	Advanced 10–8	Proficient 7–5	Basic 6–3	Minimal 2–1
Organization	Information is written with a well organized structure and clear language.	Information is written with a well organized structure, but without clear language.	The language is clear, but has no organized structure	There is neither clear language nor organized structure.
Searching	Different kinds of sources are drawn from, such as the Internet, books, and people.	Some sources are used.	Only one source is used.	No sources are used.
Obtained Knowledge	The work shows a complete understanding of the assigned homework.	The work shows substantial understanding of the assigned homework	The work shows some understanding of the assigned homework.	The work shows a lack of understanding of the assigned homework.
TOTAL				

AUTHOR

Hilal Köksal

Primary Education Department

Boğaziçi University

5 POWER OF CONGRUENT TRIANGLES

INTRODUCTION

Geometrical knowledge is applied in our surroundings to make our lives easier and safer. Civil engineers and architects use geometrical knowledge of congruence to strengthen structures against outside forces, such as winds, hurricanes, and weight. Specifically, they prefer mostly congruent triangles, since some properties of triangles allow them to reach their goals. Congruent triangles serve to brace structures. That is why this project is called Power of Congruent Triangles. The main objective of this project is to have students explore the congruence postulates of triangles, such as side–side–side (SSS), side–angle–side (SAS), angle–side–angle (ASA), and angle–angle–side (AAS), and to apply these postulates in real–life conditions, such as designing and constructing a bridge. While exploring these postulates and related software, the students will come to realize the difference between similar and congruent triangles through their own spatial reasoning. For example, they will see that angle–angle–angle (AAA) does not work for proving the congruency of triangles. In addition, through the integration of mathematics with technology, the students will discover properties of congruent triangles by engaging in some transformation activities.

OBJECTIVES

Mathematics

– Students are expected to classify the properties of triangles.

– Students are expected to use critical attributes to define congruence.

– Students are expected to use geometric concepts and properties with spatial reasoning to solve problems in fields such as engineering.

– Students are expected to identify postulates of congruence.

– Students are expected to prove congruence of two triangles by two column statements.

Technology

– Students are expected to use appropriate technology terminology according to the task.

– Students are expected to evaluate product for relevance to the task.

– Students are expected to use internet to search settings.

MATERIALS

– Computer for each student

– GSP software for each computer

– Compasses for each student

– Straightedges for each students

– Toothpicks and sticks

STUDENT INTRODUCTION

Our surroundings are full of different geometrical shapes. When you look at nature, you can see different geometrical patterns, such as honeycombs. These are constructed in a regular hexagon by bees. When you look at human–made objects, again you can see different geometrical shapes: doors, windows, domes, walls, carpets, and the like. Some of these address our aesthetic pleasure as ornamentation, and some of them are used to make our lives easier and safer. Most of us do not know how a geometrical shape might save our lives. However, engineers and architects are aware of this. Actually, some properties of these shapes enable them to make our lives safer.

An engineer is employed to construct a new bridge across a river. The old bridge was severely damaged, so it has become very dangerous for people who want to pass over it. When an engineer went to determine what type of new bridge would be useful and how to keep its price low, he or she did not have length measurement tools. Due to this lack, the engineer needs to apply his or her knowledge of geometry so that he or she will be able to estimate the length of the new bridge. In your opinion, how can the engineer measure the distance of the planned new bridge? In addition, how should the bridge be strengthened, while it is being constructed? Think of yourself as that engineer, and design and construct a model of your bridge. Use your technology and geometry skills to do that.

ENGAGEMENT

The teacher begins the discussion by asking about the geometrical shapes students see in their surroundings and in nature. After getting some answers, the teacher shows some examples of geometrical shapes from nature and human made structures, using pictures from the web site located at https://www.google.com.tr/search?q=bridge+designing&hl=tr&prmd=imvns&tbm=isch&tbo=u&source=univ&sa=X&ei=uyoaUNXXGYzSsgbf8YGACQ&sqi=2&ved=0CFkQsAQ&biw=1024&bih=475.

Then, the teacher opens a new discussion about the functions of these structures, followed by a discussion of why these structures are woven with geometrical shapes. During the discussion, the teacher emphasizes the tasks of engineers. Their main task is to produce or construct new things in order to solve real–life problems to make people's lives easier and safer. Using a video from the web site located at http://archive.org/details/sf121, the teacher opens a new discussion about the reasons for the collapse of the Tacoma Narrows Bridge. After the video, the teacher emphasizes the use of triangles in these structures to strengthen them. This part will take one class period.

EXPLORATION

The next time the teacher meets with the students, he or she will present the story in the student introduction part above. Then, the teacher divides students into groups of three. Each group is asked to do internet research on types of bridges. They are asked to record their results in their journals and then to try to understand how two triangles are congruent by experimenting them with rods and other objects. They will record their experiments and explore the congruence postulates, SSS, SAS, ASA, and AAS. (This activity will be based on Piaget's theory, which says that cognitive and intellectual development occur in large part through manipulation of and interaction with the environment. In addition, it is easier to transmit abstract spatial reasoning using concrete materials.) Then, the students will determine whether or not their postulates work in proving congruence by applying them to paper using compasses. At the end of the activity, students will present their findings according to rubric 1 in the evaluation part. This activity should take two class periods.

EXPLANATION

So far, the students have learned the importance of congruent triangles in constructing bridges and how they can determine whether or not two triangles are congruent by engaging in hands–on activities with concrete materials by finding some congruence postulates. In this part, the students will construct congruent triangles using the Geometer's Sketchpad (GSP). In addition, they will check the validity of their congruence postulates using GSP activities.

The teacher asks the students to follow the steps below to construct a triangle that is congruent to $\triangle ABC$ using GSP.

Step 1: Construct DE so that it is congruent to AB.

Step 2: Construct a circle with radius length AC and center D.

Step 3: Construct a circle with radius length BC and center E.

Step 4: Label the intersection of the two circles F.

Step 5: Draw $\triangle DEF$. By the SSS Congruence Postulate, $\triangle DEF \cong \triangle ABC$.

Hint: First, select segment AB and point D and then construct a circle with center point D. By labeling segment AB, you will construct a circle whose radius is equal to segment AB. After constructing the circle, you should label the intersection of the line and the circle. This new point is F. Then select F and segment AC and again construct a circle. The radius of the new circle will be congruent to Side AC.

Next, place a point at the intersection of the two circles and construct the radius of the second circle. This radius is congruent to Side AC. After hiding the two circles, you have a broken triangle with two congruent sides and one congruent angle. With the two circles hidden, you need to have third congruent side to complete the congruent triangle. As you think, again construct a circle with radius equal to the length of BC. If you want to check whether you have followed the procedures correctly, drag Angle A so that you can see that when the original triangle becomes smaller, the other one becomes smaller. If it becomes bigger, the second one becomes bigger. Students will apply their GSP skills in order to control other postulates such as ASA, SAS and AAS.

EXTENTION

If there are talented students who always finish early, use this GSP activity related to transformations. Through this activity, students will be able to deepen their knowledge of congruence. In addition, since the activity sheet contains s grid, students will be able to see the coordinates of points and angles and hence develop the corresponding parts concept. Since the activity provides a facility for shape animation, the students will be able to imagine easily and visually what corresponding sides and vertices exactly matching means. In addition, students can explore the properties of congruent triangles, in particular, the reflexive, transitive, and symmetric properties.

EVALUATION

True or False

Circle the correct answer

1. To determine whether two triangles are congruent, information in each side and each angle must be given. [True or False]

2. Since congruent triangles have the same shape, their corresponding angles are congruent. [True or False]

3. Two triangles are congruent if their vertices can be matched so that the corresponding parts (sides and angles) of the triangles are congruent. [True or False]

4. The SSA postulate can be used to prove the congruence of two triangles. [True or False]

5. For two triangles to have congruent interior angles is sufficient for proving congruence of the two triangles. [True or False]

6. Every triangle is congruent to itself. [True or False]

7. When checking if your construction of a triangle is congruent to an original one in GSP, you should drag one corner of your construction so the original triangle moves together with the second one. [True or False]

8. When a bridge is being built, properties of congruence are applied to make strong, stable structures. [True or False]

9. Two triangles with two sides and a non–included angle equal may or may not be congruent. [True or False]

10. Congruence of two triangles is proved using two–column statements. [True or False]

Answer Sheet

1) F, 2) T, 3) T, 4) F, 5) F, 6) T, 7) F, 8) T, 9) T, 10) T

Short Answer

1) Are △RPQ and △MNQ congruent? Why?

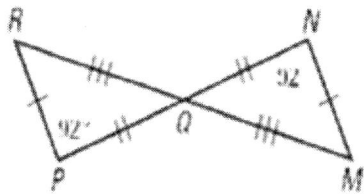

2) Identify the correct congruence statement.

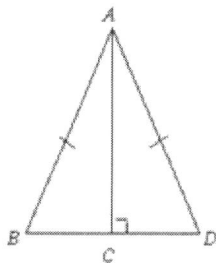

3) Complete the proof.

Given: Side BC ≅ Side DA, Angle 1 ≅ Angle 2

Prove: △BEA ≅ △DEC

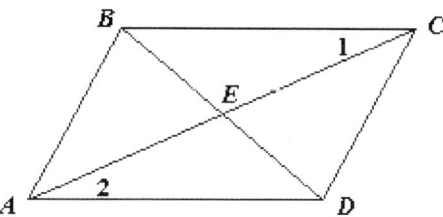

Side BC ≅ Side DA and Angle 1 ≅ Angle 2, so ΔBCA ≅ ΔDAC by SAS. Then, since (a) _____, Side BE ≅ Side DE, Side AE ≅ Side CE. Angle BEA ≅ Angle DEC by (b) _____, so ΔBEA ≅ ΔDEC by (c)_____

4) A common way to prove that two segments or two angles are congruent is to show that they are _____ parts of congruent triangles.

5) The angle between two sides is_____ and the side between two angles is _____

Answer Sheet

1) Yes, they are congruent by the SSS and SAS postulates.

2) AAS

3) a) Side BA ≅ Side CD; b) vertex angle; c) SSS

4) Corresponding

5) Included angle and included side

Multiple Choice Questions

1) If ΔKLM ≅ ΔXYZ is NOT true, then

a) Side KM ≅ Side XZ

b) Side LM ≅ Side YX

c) Angle K ≅ Angle X

d) Angle M ≅ Angle Z

2) Use the information given in the diagram. Prove why each statement is true.

I. Side AC ≅ Side AC

II. Side AD ≅ Side BC

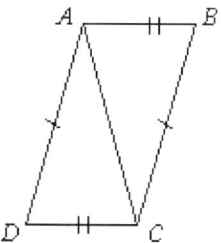

a) Given; reflexive property

b) Reflexive property; given

c) Reflexive property; reflexive property

d) Transitive property; given

3) Angle CBA ≅ ?

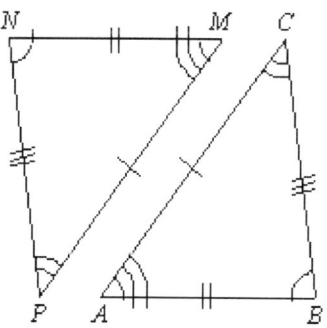

a) Angle NMP

b) Angle PNM

c) Angle PMN

d) Angle NPM

4) From the information in the diagram, can you prove that △FDG and △FDE are congruent? Explain.

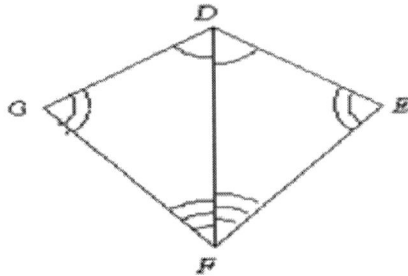

a) Yes; AAA

b) Yes; ASA

c) Yes; SSS

d) No

5) Use the figure below. Which statement is true?

Side TV ≅ Side XV, Side UV ≅ Side VW

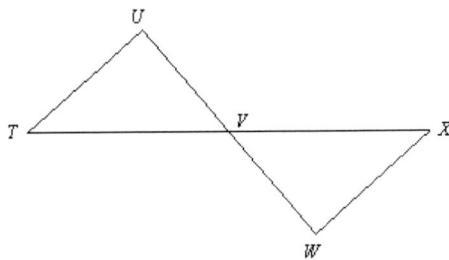

a) △TUV ≅ △VWX by ASA

b) △TUV ≅ △VWX by SAS

c) △TUV ≅ △XWV by SAS

d) △TUV ≅ △XWV by ASA

6) Determine which triangles are congruent by AAS using the information in the diagram below.

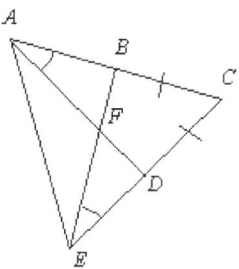

a) △ABF ≅ △EDF

b) △ADC ≅ △EBC

c) △ABE ≅ △EDA

d) △ABE ≅ △CBE

7) What else must you know to prove the triangles congruent for the reason shown?

1− ASA

2− SAS

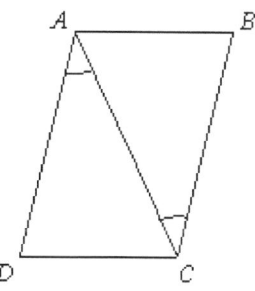

a) Angle ADC ≅ Angle ABC; Side AD ≅ Side BC

b) Side AD ≅ Side BC

c) Angle ACD ≅ Angle CAB ≅ Angle ACD; Side AB ≅ Side CD

d) Side AD ≅ Side BC; Angle ACD ≅ Angle CAB

8) Given triangle ≅ DEF, if Side DE ≅ Side EF and Angle E = 30, what is the measure of Angle F?

a) 79

b) 75

c) 71

d) 67

9) Given that Angle ECA ≅ Angle EAC, what other information would NOT help you prove that Side BA ≅ Side DC?

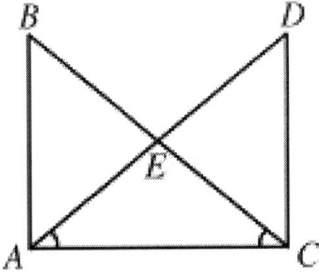

a) Angle B ≅ Angle D

b) Side EB ≅ Side ED

c) Side BC ≅ Side DA

d) Side ED ≅ Side EC

10) The two triangles are congruent. Find the missing side lengths and missing angle measures.

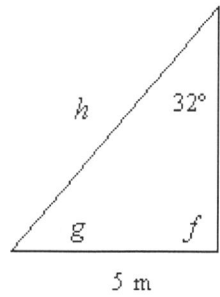 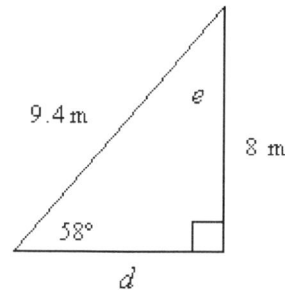

a) d = 5 m; e = 32 degrees; f = 90 degrees; g = 58 degrees; h = 5 m

b) d = 8 m; e = 32 degrees; f = 90 degrees; g = 58 degrees; h = 9.4 m

c) d = 5 m; e = 32 degrees; f = 90 degrees; g = 58 degrees; h = 9.4 m

d) d = 5 m; e = 32 degrees; f = 58 degrees; g = 90 degrees; h = 5 m

Answer Sheet

1) B, 2) B, 3) B 4) B 5) C 6) B 7) B 8) B 9) B 10) C

ALTERNATIVE ASSESSMENT

The teacher can use this project to assess the students' learning after the instructions. The project will be an indicator of the students' conceptual understanding. In addition, the teacher can easily see the students' connections of geometrical knowledge to real–life conditions. (NCTM, Process Standards, Connection). The teacher will assess the process of the project, as well as its product. The students will develop their problem–solving skills, their research methods, their reasoning and proof skills, and their representation and communication skills. Therefore, this project serves as an alternative assessment of their knowledge of Congruent Triangles, as well as a method for preparing students for real–life situations. In addition, the students will acquire or develop higher–order thinking and cooperative–working skills.

This project consists of three tasks. Since the process is important for the ongoing assessment, these tasks will be evaluated separately.

Task 1

It is very important to see as many different alternatives as possible in order to make the best decision for completing the project. Therefore, your first task will be to research types of bridges around the world. You will probably want to use the Internet for this task for distant countries, and you can visit important bridges in your own area and take photographs from different points of view. In addition, you should research the appropriateness of bridges for their geographical locations. You can give examples of important famous bridges of various kinds. You will prepare a poster for this task. Details of the task are in the following rubric.

Rubric 1: Classroom Study Poster

	Technical Structure	**Content**	**Team work**
4–3	The appearance of the poster is very structured, the fonts have the appropriate size, the color of the background is well adjusted, and the visual representations are appropriate for the content.	Four or five different types of bridges have been considered, geographical features for each bridge are given, each type of bridge has at least one example, photographs or pictures for each type are accessible, the types of materials used for constructing them are provided, the student evaluates the example bridges with respect to their appropriateness for their geographical placement and materials.	Each member of the group has worked on some aspect of the poster, the group members have visited the bridges together, and they have met as a group at least once.
2–1	The appearance of the poster is good, the fonts are appropriate for the size of the poster, but somewhere they have different sizes, or the background color disturbs the eyes.	Two or three different types of bridges have been considered, some have only one example, photographs or pictures are accessible, or the type of material for building them is not available.	Some members have not participated actively, or they have met only once as a group.
0–1	The appearance of the poster is not neat, or fonts are not consistent with each other.	Only one or two types of bridges have been considered, there are no non–local examples, or the photographs or pictures of the bridges are not relevant in our context.	There is no evidence of team spirit.

Task 2

In this activity, you will design one type of bridge. While designing it, you will use equipment such as compasses, straightedges, rulers, and protractors. The students' work will be evaluated according to the following rubric.

	Investigation	Plan	Hands–on drawings
4–3	The student understands the task completely, and uses a variety of working techniques, such as technological or scientific.	Different types of designs are considered, comparisons are made between them, and appropriate equipment and tools are used without errors.	The drawings are neat and clear, there is no confusion in them, and the drawings are appropriate to our subject, congruent triangles, and have been completed accurately.
2–1	Some parts of the task are missing, limited resources are used, or the approach to the problem is very simple.	There is thinking about only one type of design, limited tools and technological resources are used, or mathematics and technology are used with errors.	The drawings are not neat, they are somehow related to congruence, or some drawings are incomplete.
0–1	There is no understanding of the task or an ineffective approach to the task.	There is no determined plan or no usage of either technology or mathematics	The drawings are completely missing or are completely irrelevant to the subject.

Task 3

In this part, you will construct two models of bridges using prior designs. The rubric for this task is below.

	Completeness	Demonstration of congruent triangles	Consistency with planned design
4–3	The model is completed.	Congruent triangles are demonstrated in the model, explanations of these congruent triangles exist in a separate report, and the postulates are there.	The model is consistent with the planned design (from rubric 2).
2–1	The model is somewhat completed.	The demonstration of congruent triangles is weak, or there is no explanation of them with respect to the postulates.	There are some parts missing from the planned design, or there are some differences from the design.
0–1	The model is not completed.	There is no demonstration of congruent triangles.	The model is completely different from the design.

	Reaching conclusions using concrete objects	Drawings	Types of bridges
4–3	Through an excellent explanation using concrete objects, the students have drawn accurate and reasonable conclusions, the postulates they used are valid, and they have come to realize that neither AAA nor SSA works for proving congruence.	The drawings are neat and clear, they support the students' conclusions, and the students have used colored pencils so the details can be seen.	Four different types of bridges are presented in the mini–demonstration, the students have researched which types of materials are used for building them, and there is an emphasis on the geometrical shapes on the bridges.
2–1	Some conclusions are accurate, the explanation is not bad, but there is no evidence of understanding of the inadequacy of AAA or SSA.	The drawings are not neat and clear, they only partially support the conclusions, or the lack of colorful drawing causes confusion.	Two or three different types of bridges are presented, there is no visual representation of the bridges, or there is only a weak connection of the bridges with geometrical shapes.
0–1	Concrete materials are used incorrectly, no valid postulates are used, or the explanation is not reasonable.	There are no meaningful drawings or no accurate usage of compasses.	At most one type of bridge is presented, or there is no reference to geometrical shapes.

AUTHOR

Yasemin Çiçek

Primary Education Department

Boğaziçi University

Made in the USA
San Bernardino, CA
24 May 2016